Freedom *from the* Seven Deadly Sins

Freedom *from the* Seven Deadly Sins

BILLY GRAHAM

W Publishing Group

An Imprint of Thomas Nelson

Freedom from the Seven Deadly Sins

© 1955, 2025 The Billy Graham Literary Foundation

All rights reserved. No portion of this book may be reproduced, stored in a retrieval system, or transmitted in any form or by any means—electronic, mechanical, photocopy, recording, scanning, or other—except for brief quotations in critical reviews or articles, without the prior written permission of the publisher.

Published in Nashville, Tennessee, by W Publishing, an imprint of Thomas Nelson.

Thomas Nelson titles may be purchased in bulk for educational, business, fundraising, or sales promotional use. For information, please email SpecialMarkets@ThomasNelson.com.

Unless otherwise noted, all Scripture quotations are taken from the New King James Version®. Copyright © 1982 by Thomas Nelson. Used by permission. All rights reserved.

Scripture quotations marked ESV are taken from the ESV® Bible (The Holy Bible, English Standard Version®). Copyright © 2001 by Crossway, a publishing ministry of Good News Publishers. All rights reserved.

Scripture quotations marked KJV are taken from the King James Bible. Public domain.

Interior Design: Kait Lamphere
Cover Design: Jamie DeBruyn

ISBN 978-1-4003-5191-6 (TP)
ISBN 978-1-4003-5192-3 (eBook)
ISBN 978-1-4003-5193-0 (audiobook)

Library of Congress Control Number: to come

Printed in the United States of America
25 26 27 28 29 LBC 5 4 3 2 1

Contents

Preface // vii
Introduction // ix

Pride // 1
Anger // 11
Envy // 23
Impurity // 35
Gluttony // 47
Laziness // 61
Greed // 73

Praying the Scriptures // 85
Endnotes // 123
About the Author // 125
Steps to Peace with God // 127

Preface

With great expectation, the release of *Freedom from the Seven Deadly Sins* is adapted from Dr. Billy Graham's popular long-running radio program *Hour of Decision*. This series was broadcast seventy years ago as God opened doors for this beloved gospel preacher to proclaim the good news of God's love and forgiveness and Christ's salvation. Lifting up God's written truth, he stepped into the global arena saying to millions of listening ears: "You have not come to hear what I have to say, but what God has to say!"

Glean from Dr. Graham's powerful points that explode with passion for living life God's way. This revered author stated, "I have never met a person at peace who practices sinful behaviors. For Pride causes us to stumble. Anger is our enemy. Envy and Greed exact a terrible price.

Freedom from the Seven Deadly Sins

Laziness defeats us. Impurity scorns. And Gluttony causes our minds to dwell on indulging earthly satisfactions. Instead, the Bible says, 'Walk in the Spirit, and you shall not fulfill the lust of the flesh' (Galatians 5:16)."

We are pleased for this book to emerge in the twenty-first century with the message that still resonates in human hearts, delivered by the most influential evangelist of the twentieth century. People from around the world come to study his work and ministry documented in every form of communication known to humanity. The historical treasury and the perpetuation of his ongoing ministry is fully displayed at the Billy Graham Archive and Research Center in Charlotte, North Carolina. His well-respected literary collection continues to declare the Word of God—that never changes—because it stands the test of time and lives on in power and grace, just as the Bible says.

*–W Publishing Group,
an imprint of Thomas Nelson*

Introduction

After a minister had spoken strongly against sin one morning, one of his members said, "We don't want you to talk so plainly about sin because if our boys and girls hear you mention it, they will more easily become sinners. Call it a mistake if you will, but do not speak so bluntly about sin."

The minister went to the medicine shelf and brought back a bottle of strychnine marked Poison. He said, "I see what you want me to do. You want me to change the label. Suppose I take off this 'poison' label and put on some mild label such as 'peppermint candy.' Can't you see the danger? The milder you make the label, the more deadly the poison."

For decades, we have been putting a mild label on sin. We've called it "error," "negative action," and "inherent fault." But it is high time that we put a Poison label back on the poison bottle and not be afraid to be as plain as the Bible is about the tragic consequences of sin.

Pope Gregory the Great, at the end of the sixth century, divided all sins under seven heads. He said that every sin that a person commits can be classified by seven words. He named the sins: pride, anger, envy, impurity, gluttony, slothfulness (laziness), and avarice (greed). They have been called down through the centuries as "the seven deadly sins." These sins are nowhere collectively mentioned in a single passage in the Bible, and yet they are all condemned separately in many places. Thomas Aquinas and most of the great theologians have agreed with Pope Gregory, and these seven deadly sins have become a recognized part of moral theology.

These sins also became the subjects of poets. The scheme of Dante Alighieri's "Purgatory" follows the order of the seven deadly sins. They are also discussed fully in Geoffrey Chaucer's "Parson's Tale" and in Christopher Marlowe's *Doctor Faustus*.

Pride

*"When pride comes, then comes shame;
but with the humble is wisdom"*
(PROVERBS 11:2).

The first of the seven deadly sins is pride. It naturally comes first—for as we read in Proverbs 16:18, "Pride goes . . . before a fall." Pride is thus the mental and moral condition that precedes almost all other sins. All sin is selfishness in some form or other, and pride consists essentially of undue self-esteem, delighting in the thought of one's own superiority over his fellows. Scripture reminds us, "Everyone proud in heart is an abomination to the LORD; though they join forces, none will go unpunished" (Proverbs 16:5). Again in Proverbs 29:23 we read, "A man's pride will bring him low, but the humble in spirit will retain honor."

The pride that God loathes is not self-respect or a legitimate sense of personal dignity. It is a haughty, undue self-esteem out of all proportion to our actual worth. It is that egotism which is repulsive to both humans and God. It is that revolting conceit which swaggers before individuals and struts in the presence of the Almighty. God hates it. It is an abomination unto Him, which means that it makes Him shudder. God has told us in Psalm 101:5, "The one who has a haughty look and a proud heart, him I will not endure." God cannot stand or endure pride. He hates it!

Pride may take various forms, but it all emanates from the haughty human heart. Some take pride in their looks, others in their race, others in their business, others in their social life. In other words, pride may be spiritual, intellectual, material, or social. The most repugnant of these four is spiritual pride. This pride of the spirit was the sin that caused Lucifer, the devil, to fall. This is where sin actually began.

We read in Isaiah 14:12–15,

> How you are fallen from heaven, O Lucifer, son of the morning! How you are cut down to the ground, you who weaken the nations!
>
> For you have said in your heart: "I will ascend into heaven, I will exalt my throne above the stars of God;

Pride may take various forms, but it all EMANATES from the haughty human *heart*.

> I will also sit on the mount of the congregation on the farthest sides of the north;
>
> "I will ascend above the heights of the clouds; I will be like the Most High."
>
> Yet you shall be brought down to Sheol, to the lowest depths of the Pit.

Here we find Lucifer saying, "I will," five times. *"I will be above God."* It was the pride of his heart that was the first sin ever committed in the universe. When we, like Lucifer, begin to feel that we are self-contained and self-sufficient, we are on dangerous ground.

Spiritual pride, because it trusts in one's own virtue rather than the grace of God, is earmarked for God's judgment. It induces in us a contempt for others and makes us contemptible to those about us. It says with the repulsive Pharisee of old, "God, I thank you that I am not as other men are." It is smug, self-satisfied, and full of conceit. God loathes spiritual pride because it presumes to be good in its own right. It is the strutting of a tramp clad in filthy rags who imagines that he is the best dressed of all men. Spiritual pride would be humorous if it wasn't so tragic. God has sounded a stern warning for these descendants of the Pharisees. He has told us in James 4:6, "God resists the proud, but gives grace to the humble."

PRIDE

There are some people who think they have a corner on the gospel. They have become conceited, smug, proud, and pharisaical. There are others that glory in their self-righteousness and think that they are better than other people. They don't do this, and they don't do that. They keep the letter of the law but have long since forgotten the spirit of the law. They are guilty of spiritual pride. There are also others who think themselves to be pure and all others impure. They have forgotten that there is no such thing as a completely pure church. Jesus taught that the chaff and the wheat would grow together, and that we would not be able to distinguish them until the end of time. Yet we have many Pharisees today going about trying to throw the chaff out of the wheat, doing that which God said could never be done until Christ comes again. We have many going about pulling specks out of other people's eyes when they have beams in their own eyes. They have a haughty, superior, "chip on the shoulder" attitude. They spend their time criticizing and gossiping about others. This is the worst pride of all.

Another form of pride is intellectual pride. The Bible says to those who suffer from this kind of spiritual delusion, "Knowledge puffs up, but love edifies. And if anyone thinks that he knows anything, he knows nothing yet as he ought to know" (1 Corinthians 8:1b–2). This kind of pride manifests itself in arrogance toward the unlearned, the illiterate, and the oppressed. It forgets that our mental capacities were given by God, and that the knowledge we attain is largely the labor of others. Is this a reason for intellectual arrogance? Paul said in Romans 12:16, "Do not set your mind on high things, but associate with the humble."

The Greek philosopher Plato (fourth century BC) once entertained some friends in a room where there was a richly ornamented couch. When Diogenes of Sinope entered Plato's house, he trampled upon his carpet, saying that he "trampled on the empty pride of Plato," to which Plato retorted, "How much arrogance are you displaying, O Diogenes! when you think that you are not arrogant all."[1]

Intellectual pride is too often the enemy of the gospel of Christ because it gives its possessor self-confidence rather than God-confidence. We read in Proverbs 3:5, "Trust in the LORD with all your heart, and lean not on your own understanding." But the intellectually proud are not like that. They like to put God in a test tube, and if He cannot be put in a test tube, then they cannot accept Him. They do not like to lean on Him and trust Him. They cannot understand that faith goes beyond learning, knowledge, and even reason, and accepts that which may not even appear logical to the mind. To have knowledge without faith is to use only half of your mind. The psalmist said in Psalm 111:10, "The fear of the LORD is the beginning of wisdom."

True religion, contrary to the conception of some, increases your intellect rather than distracts from it. Paul, himself an intellectual, said in Romans 12:2, "Be transformed by the renewing of your mind." The kind of intellectual pride that is given to intolerance, bigotry, and smugness, God hates. God abhors intellectual pride. He says in Proverbs 26:12, "Do you see a man wise in his own eyes? There is more hope for a fool than for him."

Still another manifestation of pride is the pride of material things. Material possessions, like other blessings, flow from God. The Lord says in Deuteronomy 8:18, "And you shall remember the LORD your God, for it is He who gives you power to get wealth." In 1 Chronicles 29:12 David said, "Both riches and honor come from You, and You reign over all. In Your hand is power and might; in Your hand it is to make great and to give strength unto all."

In material pride, self is enthroned instead of God. Secondary things are exalted to a place of first importance, and life gets out of balance.

In material *pride*, self is ENTHRONED instead of God. Secondary things are EXALTED to a place of first importance, and life gets out of *balance*.

The individual then begins to concentrate on what he or she has rather than on what he or she is in the sight of God, and the soul begins to shrivel. Material pride tends to make one covetous. The lust for money can be more habit-forming than the thirst for drink. We are warned in Psalm 62:10, "Do not trust in oppression, nor vainly hope in robbery; if riches increase, do not set your heart on them." The Bible again warns in 1 Timothy 6:9, "Those who desire to be rich fall into temptation and a snare, and into many foolish and hurtful lusts which drown men in destruction and perdition."

All the material things that you have come from God. The ability to accumulate wealth comes from God. The time you are allotted to enjoy material things comes from God. So why all this unjustified human pride of your possessions? James 1:17 teaches: "Every good gift and every perfect gift is from above." You have absolutely nothing that you did not receive from God. He gave you the strength to work, a mind to think, and opportunities to thrive. It all came from God.

Then there is social pride. This manifests itself in class, racial, and caste arrogance. A statesman has said that the tiny atom made us all the same size. God does not make the distinctions in people that people make between themselves.

There are few individuals today who really believe in

the super race. The idea of a super race is not biblical, not scriptural, and not Christian. While touring Germany I heard a great deal about Adolf Hitler, who believed in a super race. His view upset the world and devastated a great nation.

How many people have social pride that is sinful? It is interesting to note on great state occasions that the ambassadors and rulers of small nations are resplendent in gold braid and glittering apparel, but the representatives of the great nations are distinguished by their modest attire. A zebra is gaudier than a workhorse, but the lowly horse is loved most because he serves us best.

Yes, the Bible teaches that pride is sin. Any kind of pride is a stumbling block to the kingdom of God. The greatest sin that will keep men and women from the kingdom of God is the sin of pride. Pride is the sin that God seemingly hates most.

What can you do about it? Confess your pride. Humble yourself in the sight of God. Come to the cross of Jesus Christ, and "Let this mind be in you which was also in Christ Jesus" (Philippians 2:5). No person will ever get to the kingdom proudly. No individual can walk up to God with pride in his or her heart and be received. You can only come to God when you humble yourself, acknowledge your sin, and receive Jesus Christ as your Savior.

Anger

"Hatred stirs up strife, but love covers all sins"
(PROVERBS 10:12).

Anger is one of humanity's most devastating sins. This is one sin that everyone is capable of committing. The tiny baby has a fit of temper and loses its dinner. The little boy has a tantrum and upsets the family decorum. The wife loses her temper and develops a sick headache. The husband gets angry and loses his appetite. Every member of the family is subject to its blight. No one is by nature immune to this dispositional disease of human nature.

Anger breeds remorse in the heart, discord in the home, bitterness in the community, and confusion in the state. Homes are often destroyed by the swirling tornadoes of heated domestic anger. Business relations are often shattered by fits of violent temper when reason gives way to venomous wrath. Friendships are often broken by the keen knife of indignation, which is sharpened by the whetstone of anger.

Anger is denounced by the church and condemned by the sacred Scriptures. It murders, assaults, and attacks—causing physical and mental harm to its victims. Its recoil, like a high-powered rifle, often hits back at the one who wields it, doing equal damage to the offender and the offended.

Because anger has brought so much unhappiness and confusion to the world, God loathes it. In Psalm 37:8 we read, "Cease from anger, and forsake wrath; do not fret—it only causes harm." Jesus condemned it in no uncertain terms and classed it with the heinous sin of murder. He said in Matthew 5:22, "I say to you that whosoever is angry with his brother without a cause shall be in danger of the judgment. And whosoever . . . says, 'You fool!' shall be in danger of hell fire." The wise Solomon said in Proverbs 16:32, "He who is slow to anger is better than the mighty, and he who rules his spirit than he who takes a city." The Bible again says in James 1:19, "So then, my beloved brethren, let every man be swift to hear, slow to speak, slow to wrath."

Anger breeds remorse in the heart, *discord* in the home, *bitterness* in the community, and *confusion* in the state.

Freedom from the Seven Deadly Sins

Anger is a heinous sin because it reveals the animal nature of humans. Many people are charming, lovable, and likable until they become obsessed with a fit of rage, and then they are transformed into repulsive, irrational creatures more like wild beasts than civilized human beings. Doctors tell us that when any human emotion is overstimulated, excessive amounts of adrenaline are supplied by nature to replenish the emotional drain on our systems. The person with a violent temper uses up this extra supply of energy to feed the flame of his or her passion rather than to put out the fire.

Anger not only brings out the animal nature of people but hinders Christian testimony. Peter, angered at the Roman soldiers, grabbed a sword and cut off the servant's ear, but Jesus reproved him for his angry spirit and said, "For all who take the sword will perish by the sword" (Matthew 26:52). Many a Christian witness has been mined by carnal anger.

A professed Christian woman was very anxious for her husband to find Christ. One day her minister spoke to her husband about his soul, and the minister was taken aback when the man said, "I'm not particularly an irreligious man, but if Christianity should make me wrathful like my wife, I want no part of it."

The minister went to the lady in question and told

ANGER

her precisely what her husband had said. She had not realized that her temper had been so out of control, and she was repentant about it. Together the minister and the woman knelt in prayer while she sobbed her heart out to God.

A few days later the husband had been out fishing. When he came into the house with his rod over his shoulder, he accidentally hit a costly lamp, which went crashing to the floor. He stood with his hands over his ears waiting for the second crash of his wife's anger—but it never came. He looked up to see his wife smiling as she said, "Don't worry about it, dear. Accidents happen in the best of families."

"You mean you're not angry as usual?" he asked.

"No, dear, that's all a thing of the past. I'm sorry I've been so impatient, but God is helping me to gain control of my temper."

A few Sundays later the husband joined the church. Her testimony had been strengthened by her anger being controlled by the Spirit of God.

Anger also causes people to lose the joy of living. We read in Genesis 4:6 about God asking Cain, whose joy had been expelled by anger, "Why are you angry? And why has your countenance fallen?" The bad thing about losing your temper is that other things are often lost with it. When temper rages, your good expression goes. When temper rages, your reputation goes. When temper rages, your friends go. When temper rages, your opportunity goes. When temper rages, your testimony goes.

Anger is the parent of murder. Cain was enraged before he murdered Abel. It cocks the assassin's pistol, dispenses the killer's poison, and sharpens the murderer's dagger. It devastates, mutilates, and destroys. It kindles the fire of passion, fans the flame of envy, and leaves the soul barren and desolate. Here, of course, we are speaking of irrational, unjustifiable anger—the kind that goads the conscience, lashes out at the innocent, and induces malice and discord in the home and in society. This kind of anger God hates.

Too many of us are guilty of this blighting sin. Though we excuse ourselves by blaming our uncontrolled anger upon our natural disposition, deep within, our conscience tells us that it is wrong. There is the haunting conviction that we are grieving the Spirit of God when we are ruled by violent temper.

What can be done about this dispositional sin? Does the Christian faith have an answer? Can Christ calm the tempestuous sea of anger as He did the turbulent Sea of Galilee long ago? If there were no way to overcome anger, if there were no way to bring it under control,

ANGER

God would never have said in Proverbs 14:29, "He who is slow to wrath has great understanding, but he who is impulsive exalts folly." God never demands an action that is impossible of achievement. There is a victory—in Christ—over sinful anger. Even the Greek philosopher Plutarch said, "I came to the opinion that this passion [anger] is not altogether incurable, for those, at least, who wish to cure it."[1]

The first step, then, in finding victory over unjustified anger is to want to get rid of it. The will comes to the forefront and says, "I *will* do something about this unruly temper of mine." This means that you stop justifying yourself by saying, "My whole family is quick-tempered—I inherited it from my mother." Or, "Everyone loses his temper some time or other—what's wrong with that?" You must recognize it as an ugly, venomous sin both in the eyes of God and in your own sight.

Secondly, we must confess this evil anger to God and ask His forgiveness for fits of rage and uncontrolled temper. If anger is a sin and if being angry with one's brother without a cause brings the judgment of God, we ought to hate it, despise it, and seek by divine methods to overcome it. In 1 John 1:9 we read, "If we confess our sins, He is faithful and just to forgive us our sins and to cleanse us from all unrighteousness."

If *anger* is a sin and if being angry with one's brother without a cause brings the JUDGMENT of God, we ought to hate it, despise it, and seek by DIVINE methods to *overcome* it.

ANGER

Anyone knows that hot, violent anger is unrighteous and not of Christ. God, in love and mercy, has promised both to forgive us of the sin of anger and to cleanse us from it. This does not imply that people become spineless, bland creatures without any spunk or spirit, but it does mean that our tempers that were used in wrath now become things of blessing. The tongue that once was used for profanity now becomes an instrument of praise. The hands that once hurt now become healing hands. The feet that once walked the pathways of violence now walk the pathways of love and service. The wild horses of passion are tamed by the Spirit and become our servants rather than our masters. That is exactly what Jesus meant when He said, "Blessed are the meek" (Matthew 5:5).

Remember Peter before the resurrection and the descent of the Holy Spirit? He swore in the camp of the enemy, denying his Lord, and became enraged at the soldiers who took Jesus into custody. His angry spirit was a poor witness for a disciple of the lowly Galilean. But after the Spirit of God came into his heart on the day of Pentecost, his temper was brought under control. Never again was his tongue employed in profanity. Never again were his hands used in violence. Never again was his voice raised in denial of his Lord. Never again were his feet found in the camp of the enemy. Peter's temper was not gone—it had been diverted to a constructive purpose. It had been bridled by the Spirit of God. Conversion to Christ had not made him weaker—it had made him a stronger man. No longer was he sinfully angry.

You can become a meek person. The word *meek* actually means that you become controlled by the Spirit of God. As a wild force tamed, so the Spirit of God can tame your tongue and tame the passions of your soul, if you surrender your heart and your life to Jesus Christ.

However, we are taught in the Bible that there is a righteous indignation that is legitimate and justified. In fact, if we do not have righteous indignation on occasion, we may actually be sinning. So, there is a type of anger that is justified and commended in the sight of God.

Now that type of anger is this: We are to be angry—we are to have righteous indignation at sin and corruption and immorality round about us. We are to have righteous indignation at the filthy material in media. We are to have righteous indignation at some of the evil corruption in high places that is uncovered from time to time. We are to have righteous indignation about the corruption in many of our cities and the criminals who walk our streets. We are to have righteous indignation against these things.

There is a third kind of anger, and that is the anger of God. In Romans 1:18 we read, "For the wrath of God is revealed from heaven against all ungodliness and unrighteousness of men, who suppress the truth in unrighteousness." Again, we read in Colossians 3:6, "Because of these things the wrath of God is coming upon the sons of disobedience." God is a holy and a righteous God, and His eyes are too pure to look upon evil. When sin is in His sight, God's holiness explodes into wrath and anger against sin.

Men and women who have not come to the cross of Christ, who have not come to acknowledge their sin and receive Him as Savior, are in for the wrath of God. There is a day of judgment coming when the holy wrath and anger of God will be exploded against the sinner who has not received His Son, Jesus Christ, as Savior. At the day of judgment when you come before God, if you have not received Christ, He will say, "Depart from Me, you cursed, into the everlasting fire prepared for the devil and his angels" (Matthew 25:41).

Envy

"You lust and do not have. You murder and covet and cannot obtain. You fight and war. Yet you do not have because you do not ask. You ask and do not receive, because you ask amiss, that you may spend it on your pleasures"

(JAMES 4:2–3).

Envy and jealousy can ruin reputations, split churches, and cause murders. Envy can shrink our circle of friends, ruin our business, and dwarf our souls. Procrastination may be the thief of time, but envy is the murderer of souls. We read in Job 5:2 that envy can kill a person (modern psychiatry bears this out): "For wrath kills a foolish man, and envy slays a simple one."

There is a Greek story about a man who killed himself through envy. His fellow citizens had erected a statue to one of their number who was a celebrated champion in the public games. But this man, a rival of the honored athlete, was so envious that he vowed that he would destroy that statue. Every night he went out into the darkness and chiseled at its base in an effort to undermine its foundation and make it fall. At last, he succeeded. It did fall—but it fell on him. He fell a victim of his own envy.

The Bible, whose counsel is wiser than any person, tells us not to be envious of the rich. In Psalm 49:16 we read, "Do not be afraid when one becomes rich, when the glory of his house is increased." Envying those who are more prosperous than we are does not add one dollar to our assets, but it bankrupts the soul. Envious people somehow feel that other people's fortunes are their misfortune, that others' successes are their failure, and that others' blessings are their curses. The irony of it all is that if he or she builds up such a case in his or her mind and soul, his or her failure is inevitable. I have never seen a person who profited in any way by being envious of others, but I have seen hundreds cursed by it.

You cannot have a full-orbed personality and harbor envy in your heart. We are told in Proverbs 14:30, "A sound heart is life to the body, but envy is rottenness to the bones." Envy is not a defensive weapon—it is an offensive instrument used in spiritual ambush.

Envious people somehow feel that other people's FORTUNES are their misfortune, that others' successes are their failure, and that others' *blessings* are their curses.

It wounds for the sake of wounding and hurts for the sake of hurting.

"Tell me," said the willow to the thorn, "why are you so envious of the clothes of those who pass by? Of what use can they be to you?"

"None whatsoever," replied the thorn. "I have no desire to wear them—I only want to tear them."

How like that thorn is the envious person—reaching out to destroy others without bringing any profit to himself.

Envy is one of the most heinous sins of the flesh and one of the most uncalled for. It is strongly denounced by the wise individuals of the ages and certainly denounced by God.

Solomon said in Proverbs 27:4, "Who is able to stand before jealousy?"

In Galatians 5:26 Paul said, "Let us not become conceited, provoking one another, envying one another."

James said, "For where envy and self-seeking exist, confusion and every evil thing are there" (James 3:16).

Sixteenth-century English philosopher and statesman Francis Bacon said, "Neither can he, that mindeth but his own business, find much matter for envy. For envy is a gadding passion, and walketh the streets, and doth not keep home."[1]

First-century Roman poet and satirist Horace said, "Than envy, Sicilian tyrants have invented no worse torture." Horace also said, "The envious grow thin while their neighbours fatten."[2]

Seventeenth-century writer Samuel Johnson said, "Envy is . . . the only passion which can never lie quiet for want of irritation."[3]

Petronius, a Roman courtier during the reign of Nero, said, "The vulture which explores our inmost liver, and drags out our heart and inmost nerves, is not the bird of whom our dainty poets talk, but those diseases of the soul, envy and wantonness."[4]

Envy, according to the Bible, is inherent in our very nature. We read in James 4:5, "The spirit that dwelleth in us lusteth to envy" (KJV). Cain envied Abel because he had found favor with God, and then he murdered Abel. Envy needs no justification to make an attack. More often than not, there is no real reason for its existence. It springs from the unregenerate human heart as naturally as weeds grow in a flower garden.

Joseph's brethren were envious of him and sold him into Egyptian slavery. They paid for their deed with a perilous famine, and in the end were forced of necessity to recognize Joseph's superiority. Their envy impoverished their lives, but the intended harm never came to Joseph.

Envy is a boomerang-like weapon that hurts the attacker more than the attacked.

Haman, envious of the sage Mordecai, pulled political strings to do away with him. So intent was he on annihilating the object of his envy that in over-anxiety he built gallows for Mordecai to hang on. His tragic story ended with these words, "So they hanged Haman on the gallows that he had prepared for Mordecai" (Esther 7:10).

How many of you have been hanged on the gallows that you made for some other person? Many an individual has died on the gallows of envy that he or she had prepared for another. Look around you! Right in your own community you know people who have been resentful toward others, cynical about God and religion, or rebellious toward their neighbors. I defy you to show me an envious person who is happy. The moment he or she began to build gallows of envy, this person became spiritually dead.

Why is envy so great a sin? Was it just a whim of God to denounce it? Did He arbitrarily forbid it just to make us miserable? Certainly not! God is interested in our total and complete development. We are told in 3 John verse 2, "Beloved, I pray that you may prosper in all things and be in health, just as your soul prospers."

Jealousy was one of the sins of Lucifer before he was

transformed into Satan. He was jealous of God's position and determined that he was going to dethrone God and put himself in God's place. God hates envy and jealousy. One of the sins that caused the death of Christ was jealousy. "For he knew that the chief priests had handed Him over because of envy" (Mark 15:10).

The Pharisees and Sadducees were jealous of the attention that Christ received. They were envious of the great crowds that flocked to hear Him, and envious because the people had made somewhat of a hero of Christ. Their jealousy burned as flames of fire in their hearts. They counseled together how they could put Him to death. The Pharisees and Sadducees were not on very good terms, and on most points and issues there was no agreement. However, because their jealousy was so great, they pooled their resources in order to stop Jesus. They forgot their own differences because their jealous hearts were out of control. Jealousy takes many forms and many deviations, but it is hated by God and helps destroy all that are guilty of it.

Envy is also forbidden because it destroys spiritual health. Envy is a devastating symptom of this thing called "original sin," which we all have. Don't think you are alone in possessing envy. Everyone is envious, to a greater or lesser degree. Even Paul, who warned Christians

Freedom from the Seven Deadly Sins

so sternly against envy, once had a great amount of it. His was spiritual envy. He was jealous of the new sect called Christians, and his envy blazed up in vehement wrath. He went everywhere persecuting and destroying Christians, but in the face of a Christian named Stephen, at whose stoning he had officiated, Paul saw a Light that he had never seen before. He found this same Light on the Damascus road. His envy was changed to fervent love and unrestrained joy. Paul—who was bitter, cynical, and envious—found a new zest in life when he turned from his envy and began serving the Savior.

If you were to find the germs of tuberculosis lurking in your body, you would spare no time, effort, or money in ruling them out. And yet many people are afflicted with this deadly, venomous envy, and they are doing nothing about it! In the eyes of God, it is as ugly and deadly as open immorality. It is one of the seventeen fleshly sins mentioned by Paul in Galatians and ranks with adultery, murder, fornication, and drunkenness (5:19–21). It is more prevalent than any of these, though the pulpit too seldom warns about its power to destroy. Though it is not forbidden by law, this vice that has infiltrated our modern life is sharply condemned by God. We are told in James 5:9, "Do not grumble against one another . . . lest you be condemned. Behold, the Judge is standing at the door!"

Envy is also forbidden because it takes the joy, HAPPINESS, and contentment out of living. It is impossible to know SERENITY and contentment as long as *jealousy* is in one's heart.

Freedom from the Seven Deadly Sins

Envy is also forbidden because it takes the joy, happiness, and contentment out of living. It is impossible to know serenity and contentment as long as jealousy is in one's heart. I have seen many lives filled with bitterness, hardness, frustration, confusion, and even physical ailments as a direct result of jealousy. Jealousy takes away the effectiveness of one's work and can certainly destroy one's service for God. It causes all types of physical disorders because of the nervous tension that it brings on.

Envy isolates one from fellowship with God. There is no possibility that a person can be received into fellowship with God if he has envy in his heart. If you are not a Christian and have never given your heart and life to Christ, it is one of the symptoms of the basic sin that separates you and your God. You must repent of sin and receive Christ as Savior before you can receive a new nature and victory over envy. If you are a Christian and have jealousy in your heart, then it means that you are out of fellowship with Christ and do not have the thrill and secret of victorious living. Since God loathes and abhors envy, He cannot bless you as long as you cling to it.

William Shakespeare was close to this truth when he said, "No, not the hangman's axe, bear half the keenness Of thy sharp envy."[5]

Envy erodes through the soil of the soul, marooning

the individual who indulges in it on an island of selfishness. In the chemistry of the spirit, no sin is so devastating, no sin can so quickly mar the sweet fellowship between humanity and God.

Envy isolates one from others. The envious person is destined to live alone. In the end, it becomes spiritual leprosy, isolating these individuals from friends and fellowship with God.

Those who are guilty of this sin are going to be judged. We are warned in the Bible that someday we shall stand before the judgment of God and give an account of all the secret thoughts of jealousy and envy that we have harbored in our heart.

Many of you are asking, "How can I get rid of this devastating sin that robs me of soul, health, and happiness?"

First, recognize that you have it. Doctors say that a case well diagnosed is half cured. Stop blaming others for your failures. Take inventory of your own soul and take positive action to get rid of the sins that have beset you. To admit a fault does not make you smaller—on the contrary, it makes you appear bigger in the eyes of others.

Second, confess your sin to God and renounce it. In 1 John 1:9 we read, "If we confess our sins, He is faithful and just to forgive us." James 5:16 says, "Confess your trespasses . . . that you may be healed." Many a person has started on the road to spiritual recovery by a straightforward confession to God. Confess your sins, renounce them, repent of them.

Third, open your heart to the regenerating grace of Christ. Envy cannot be overcome in your strength. Paul learned this secret and said, "I can do all things through Christ who strengthens me" (Philippians 4:13). As the Christ-nature unfolds in your life, you will find that the old strivings, the old envies, are more easily conquered. You will discover the full meaning of the words, "And those who are Christ's have crucified the flesh with the passions and desires" (Galatians 5:24), and that "the fruit of the Spirit is love, joy, peace, longsuffering" (v. 22).

Fourth, ask the Holy Spirit to come into your heart to give you victory. It is possible to "reckon yourselves to be dead indeed unto sin, but alive to God" (Romans 6:11). "The fruit of the Spirit is love" (Galatians 5:22), and where love dwells in all of its fullness, there is no room for envy and jealousy.

You can have complete and unqualified victory by surrendering completely to Christ.

Impurity

*"Create in me a clean heart, O God, and
renew a steadfast spirit within me"*
(PSALM 51:10).

The sin of impurity at the outset does not appear ugly and venomous. It comes in the guise of beauty, symmetry, and desirability. There is nothing repulsive about it. Satan clothes his goddess of lust as an angel of love, and her appearance has deceived the strongest of men. "After all, it's a natural instinct," says the rationalist. "This is God-endowed." But wait a minute—the Bible says in Proverbs 6:32–33, "Whoever commits adultery with a woman lacks understanding; he that does so destroys his own soul. Wounds and dishonor he will get, and his reproach will not be wiped away."

God hates this sin of impurity. It has caused nations

to fall. It has repeatedly ruined the sanctity of the home. It has hindered the health and development of the personality, and it has caused the spiritual impotence of thousands. It has filled our divorce courts, made thousands of innocent children homeless, and has wrecked the hope of the bright tomorrow for many a young person.

Impurity is one of the most revolting of sins because it twists and distorts one of God's most precious gifts to humankind—love—and drags it down to the level of the beast. But despite its heinousness, impurity is the most prevalent of all of Satan's contrivances. Its raucous sound falls upon our ears throughout the day in the form of filthy stories, suggestive remarks, and open vulgarity. It bids for our attention from all forms of media.

Impurity obviously has a better press agent than purity. Purity by the rank and file is considered smug, but impurity is considered smart. This is the biggest "bill of goods" that the devil ever put over on people. In selling "sex" wholesale, the momentary thrill is played up, but the consequences of this vicious sin are played down. Satan fails to speak of the remorse, the futility, the loneliness, and the spiritual devastation that go hand in hand with immorality. Nothing is said of the broken homes, the shattered lives, the fevered brains, and the diseased bodies that result from living impurely.

Impurity is one of the most REVOLTING of sins because it twists and distorts one of God's most precious gifts to humankind—*love*—and drags it down to the level of the beast.

Ask the often divorced person if a change of mates has brought any change of heart or inner peace! Ask those who are paying physically for breaking the seventh commandment if sin brings happiness! As they watch the sands of time run out, and as the folly of their youth takes its toll, their voices say eloquently, "The wages of sin is death" (Romans 6:23).

The sin of immorality is one of hell's keenest weapons for the destruction of souls, and Satan has used it effectively from the dawn of creation to this present hour. It never seems to lose its subtlety at the beginning or its destructiveness at the end. Its beauty is exceeded only by its deadliness.

A well-known American writer once wrote an article entitled, "I Am Sick of Sex." By this she meant that she was sick of seeing it everywhere. She said, "Whether I look at a newsstand or watch my television screen, it's there before me." But apparently millions of Americans do not agree with this woman. A magazine editor told me that in order to sell magazines he had to put "sex" on the front cover. In my opinion sex is probably America's greatest sin. It has gripped and paralyzed our youth, with an estimated 55 percent of male and female teens having had sexual intercourse by age eighteen.[1]

For years, we have been taught that morals were

relative and not absolute. Humanism and behaviorism laughed at the Ten Commandments and the idea of God. They taught that people were only animals, and our young people were urged to give free expression to their passions and feelings. Our high school and college young people were told that impurity is no longer wrong. The sin of "scarlet" turned to a mild pink, and a young man and woman who tried to live pure lives were laughed at and scorned even by some educational authorities. No wonder our world has plunged into an unprecedented immoral spree that threatens the very structure of our society!

There are three facts about the sin of impurity that I would like for you to notice.

First, the sin of impurity marks a person. In the days of slavery, a slave could be identified by the marks of his or her master. When individuals become mastered by sin, it is inescapable that the marks of sin are upon them. The reddened eyes and bloated cheeks of the alcoholic, the nervous twitch of those on illegal drugs, and the haughty look of the proud are all outward signs. Immorality, which is the sin of perversion and unnaturalness, has a way of making those who harbor it unnatural appearing. The shifty eye, the embarrassed blush, the suggestive glance—these are all marks of the impure. They are the outward signs of inward impurity.

But the outward marks are slight compared to the blemishes that impurity etches on the personality and upon the soul. Guilt complexes and bad consciences are fashioned in the fires of lustful passion. Out of unbalanced practices of impurity grow phobias that alarm even our most skilled psychiatrists. But worse than all, impurity mars the soul. The Bible says in Galatians 5:19, "The works of the flesh evident, which are: adultery, fornication, uncleanness, and lewdness." The Bible says that the sin of impurity is the result of the deceitfulness of sin, and teaches that "there is none who does good, no, not one" (Psalm 14:3), and that the entire human race has been tainted by the disease of sin.

The Bible also teaches that those who are guilty of this sin of impurity shall not inherit the kingdom of God. Jesus interpreted the seventh commandment—which says, "You shall not commit adultery" (Exodus 20:14)—when He said, "Whoever looks at a woman to lust for her has already committed adultery with her in his heart" (Matthew 5:28). Jesus said that a person can be guilty of this sin by thought and word, as well as deed. There are thousands today who are guilty, whose souls have been marred by the sin of impurity, and who have become separated from God because of this besetting sin.

There are *thousands* today who are guilty, whose SOULS have been marred by the sin of IMPURITY, and who have become separated from *God* because of this besetting sin.

Next, impurity mocks or deceives. Paul, writing to Titus, indicated that even he knew the deceitfulness of immorality before he came to know Jesus Christ: "For we ourselves were also foolish, disobedient, deceived, serving various lusts and pleasures" (Titus 3:3). The sin of impurity has deceived kings, prophets, sages, and saints. Do not think for one moment that you are immune to its blight! Even the wise Solomon, who through experience had every reason to know, said, "Fools mock at sin" (Proverbs 14:9).

Too many people underestimate the power of impurity. Samson toyed with it, made sport of it, and thought he had it under control, but in the end, it controlled him and ruined his life. David, chosen of God, came under its subtle spell and in a moment of weakness was deceived by the overcoming powers of impurity—and he was years climbing back to God up the steep stairway of repentance. Homes have been lost in a fleeting moment of weakness, kingdoms have been bartered for a transient pleasure, and an eternal heritage has been squandered for an hour of hell's diversion.

Impurity mocks those who harbor it in their hearts. Impurity mocks when its harvest is gathered. In Galatians 6:7–8 we read, "Do not be deceived, God is not mocked; for whatever a man sows, that he will also reap. For he who sows to his flesh will of the flesh reap corruption."

Impurity, when it is finished, brings forth remorse.

IMPURITY

Some of the most miserable people I know are those who are haunted by the memory of the wasted, wanton years of impurity. God is willing to forgive them, but they are not willing and able to forgive themselves. The magnitude of their sin has grown through the years, and it has born its fruit of regret and remorse. They have sown to the flesh, and of the flesh have reaped corruption. Their impurity mocks them, haunts them, and derides them. Like every other device of the devil, it has taken away from them all that is good and has given them nothing in return. Satan drives a hard bargain!

Then, impurity masters. The Bible says in Romans 6:16, "Do you not know that to whom you present yourselves slaves to obey, you are that one's slaves to whom you obey, whether of sin leading to death, or of obedience leading to righteousness?" Many people are mastered by impurity because they have given themselves to impurity.

A medical doctor in London accepted Christ during one of my crusades. Before his conversion he was ruled by animal passion and was dedicated to a life of unchastity. His reading room was crammed full of salacious and suggestive literature and photographs. But after his conversion he was repulsed by the thought of impure practices and promptly gathered up all his lewd literature, carried it to a London bridge, and cast it into the Thames River.

Having experienced the new birth, he yielded himself to a new Master—Jesus Christ. He became one of the most active Christian laymen in the city of London.

Thousands of people are held in the iron grip of impurity and immorality. Sin, because they have obeyed it and yielded to it, has become their master. "Whoever commits sin is a slave of sin" (John 8:34). They are conscious that what they are doing is wrong, but they are powerless to break with their impurity. Their sin has lost its keen edge of enjoyment and has settled down to a kind of bondage. It has become their master! Once they had sin—but now their sin has them!

Is there any hope for those who are held in the grip of impurity? Ah yes, there is. Mary Magdalene, the woman at Jacob's well, and the woman taken in adultery can all sing in unison:

> *There is a fountain filled with blood,*
> *Drawn from Immanuel's veins.*
> *And sinners plunged beneath that flood,*
> *Lose all their guilty stains.*[2]

There is a crimson cure for the scarlet sin.

When the adulteress was brought to Jesus by the Pharisees, they demanded that she be stoned and destroyed.

IMPURITY

Jesus stooped down and with His finger wrote on the ground. Whatever He wrote (and it well might have been the Ten Commandments) made them leave one by one. Jesus stood alone with the woman, and He asked her, "Has no one condemned you?" She said, "No one, Lord." Jesus said to her, "Neither do I condemn you; go and sin no more" (John 8:10–11). This impure woman was the symbol of all those who are held in the grip of impurity. She had sinned, yes, but "all have sinned and fall short of the glory of God" (Romans 3:23).

When Christ died on the cross, He died for the sin of impurity, as well as for other sins. Actually, impurity is only a symptom of the "original sin" that David said he was born and shaped in. Every person who is born is born a sinner. There is only one place of forgiveness, and that is at the foot of the cross where we come by repentance and faith to receive Christ as Savior. It is only on the grounds of the death of His Son that God can forgive sin.

If you bring your life to Jesus Christ, God will forgive every sin you have ever committed. He can even forget that you have ever sinned. You can be justified in His presence and cleansed of all impurity. Not only so, but He gives victory over it! He said to the woman, "Go and sin no more." There are many of you who say, "I've tried a thousand times, but it has an unbreakable grip on me."

Yes, but Jesus gave hope to this woman that He could give her victory over future sin. He never told anyone to do something but that He gave the power to do it.

You, too, can determine by God's grace that you will never commit this sin again. You have no strength of your own, but Christ will come into your heart and give you supernatural strength and power to resist the fearful temptation of passion. For the sin of impurity your conscience goads you, your memory haunts you, and society condemns you—but Jesus Christ will save you. He can be yours. Confess your sins, receive Him, and let Him cleanse you and make you a new person.

Gluttony

*"Why do you spend money for what is not
bread, and your wages for what does not satisfy?
Listen carefully to Me, and eat what is good,
and let your soul delight itself in abundance"*

(ISAIAH 55:2).

I knew a man who weighed nearly three hundred pounds. He ate more than anyone I had ever known. One time I had breakfast with him, and he ate an entire lemon chiffon pie. When I mentioned that he should lose some weight, he gave a hearty laugh and put an extra pat of butter on his toast. This man was guilty of the sin the Bible calls "gluttony."

Today most individuals live at ease with more leisure time on their hands and more food to eat than any other time period. As a result, creeping materialism (the cult of comfort) is growing by leaps and bounds. Prosperity and plenty, which advocates ease and luxury, preaches that we can live by bread alone. Appetite is its god; the merchandise counter, its altar. Its creed is plenty, and its heaven is comfort. In an era of economic prosperity, there is a grave danger of the sin of indulging our fleshly appetites and yielding to inordinate eating, drinking, and revelry.

Gluttony is one of the seven deadly sins and was placed by the church fathers right alongside pride, envy, and impurity. It is a sin that most of us commit, but few of us mention. Although there are no laws on our statute books that forbid gluttony, it is strongly denounced in the Bible.

Many people guilty of gluttony are quick to condemn others for their sins. They can readily detect a mote of impurity in the other person but remain ignorant of the beam of overindulgence in themselves. It is easy for individuals who surfeit and stuff their bodies with needless delicacies to look at others who overdrink and say like the Pharisee of old, "God, I thank You that I am not like other men—extortioners, unjust, adulterers, or even as this tax collector" (Luke 18:11). It is easy for individuals who are enslaved by his or her stomach to condemn the person who is enslaved by drink. But in God's sight, sin is sin.

Gluttony, gorging, and overindulgence are condemned

GLUTTONY

as sharply as the other deadly sins that plague people. Philippians 3:19 reads, "Whose end is destruction, whose god is their belly, and whose glory is in their shame—who set their mind on earthly things." Here gluttony is identified with materialism, "who set their mind on earthly things."

Gluttony is a sin, first, because it is a physical expression of the philosophy of materialism. It laughs at righteous restraint and scorns temperance and decency. It cries, "Eat, drink and be merry, for tomorrow we die." It makes no room for God and has no consideration for eternity. It lives for the present, and its philosophy is, "You live only once, so live it up."

Jesus gave us a classic example of a man who lived for this life only. In his prosperity he said, "I will pull down my barns and build greater, and there will I store all my crops and my goods. And I will say to my soul, 'Soul, you have many goods laid up for many years; take your ease; eat, drink, and be merry" (Luke 12:18–19). His philosophy was little different from our materialistic philosophy of today. Build bigger . . . take it easier . . . drink more . . . eat more . . . enjoy life more.

We hear this philosophy blaring out of our radio and television sets from morning till night. The accent is on comfort, ease, and the satisfying of our appetites.

Gluttony is a sin, first, because it is a physical expression of the philosophy of MATERIALISM. It laughs at righteous RESTRAINT and scorns *temperance* and decency.

GLUTTONY

Everywhere we are encouraged to easier living and more and better—with the accent on the things of this world. Temperance, restraint, and self-discipline are being forgotten in the rush toward ease and plenty. This materialistic philosophy is trying in vain to drink its way to happiness, fight its way to peace, spend its way to prosperity, and enjoy its way to heaven. How easy it is to fill our minds with rubbish, our stomachs with trash, and starve our souls. God has said in Deuteronomy 8:3, "Man shall not live by bread alone; but man lives by every word that proceeds from the mouth of the LORD."

Gluttony is a perversion of a natural, God-given appetite. We must fix in our minds the fact that sin is not always flagrant and open transgression. It is often the perversion and distortion of natural, normal desires and appetites. Love is often distorted into lust. Self-respect too often is perverted into godless ambition. When a God-given, normal hunger for things is extended greedily into abnormality so that it harms the body, dulls the mind, and stultifies the soul, it becomes sin. In Proverbs 23:21 we read, "For the drunkard and the glutton will come to poverty, and drowsiness will clothe a man with rags."

The gratification of our fleshly appetites is not to receive first importance in our lives. Jesus said, "Therefore do not worry, saying, 'What shall we eat?' or 'What shall we drink?' or 'What shall we wear?' . . . But seek first the kingdom of God and His righteousness, and all these things shall be added to you" (Matthew 6:31, 33).

Most of us have disregarded Jesus' warning about putting our fleshly appetites first. Too many of us spend our lives in the pursuit of the material, crowding Christ out altogether; and then in the last frenzied, hurried moment of life we cry, "God have mercy on my soul!" I ask you: Is it fair, is it intelligent, to wait until the last second of life upon this earth to transact life's most urgent business—settling your account with God? Of course it is not fair, and I seriously doubt the genuineness of such a deathbed repentance. God may give a person a chance on his or her deathbed to repent of sin if the person has never been warned and has never heard the plan of salvation clearly explained. But to a person who has deliberately rejected Christ and continued to sin, there is little hope that this individual can find peace with God in his or her last hours. The Bible warns that a day will come when a person seeks God but will not find Him and call on God but He will not hear.

Many people do not look upon gluttony as a vicious sin, and yet it is condemned from one end of the Bible to the other. When we go to the table, we show no self-restraint and no self-discipline; we eat our way not only to the grave, but to hell and destruction as well. Of course, gluttony is not only the sin of overeating food or drink. It can be the sin of ambition, greed, or lust. Gluttony can also be indulged in by married couples who do not use self-restraint and temperance in their relations with each other. They have overindulged, and as a result their bodies as well as their minds and souls suffer. The Bible demands that in all things we are to be temperate, and we are not to abuse any God-given privilege.

Gluttony is the epitome of human selfishness. It is destined to be judged like any other deadly sin. God says in Amos 6:3–4, 6, "Woe to you . . . who lie on beds of ivory, stretch out on your couches, eat lambs from the flock and calves from the midst of the stall; . . . who drink wine from bowls, and anoint yourselves with the best ointments."

Forty-four percent of the world live in squalor, misery, and hunger. Too long have the privileged few exploited and ignored the underprivileged billions of the world. Our selfishness is at long last catching up with us. Unless we begin to act, to share, and to do something about this great army of starving humanity, God will judge us. Unless Christians break with their selfishness and begin to help these billions of starving people out of their misery, they will turn to other political and social alternatives.

Our *selfishness* is at long last catching up with us. Unless we begin to ACT, to SHARE, and to DO something about this great army of starving *humanity*, God will judge us.

GLUTTONY

Even though this is an era of prosperity, there is shocking evidence of selfishness and greed on every hand. Who knows but what God has permitted this prosperity to come that we may share it with the suffering and needy and thus lure them by our love and compassion! First John 3:17 speaks for itself: "Whoever has this world's goods, and sees his brother in need, and shuts up his heart from him, how does the love of God abide in him?"

We are not only to witness for Christ with our lips, but with our hands—hands laden with food for the hungry, clothes for the naked, and water for the thirsty. We read in 1 John 3:18, "My little children, let us not love in word or in tongue, but in deed and in truth." Shame, O shame, that in an hour when billions of people are hanging in the balance between Christian love and the clutches of materialism, we should be given to surfeiting, gluttony, and drunkenness! May God awaken us out of our sinful stupor before it is too late!

Gluttony is sinful because it defiles the body, which is the temple of the Holy Spirit. Our bodies were not created to be dissipated and abused by sin—they were created by God Himself and were intended to be the dwelling of His Spirit. The Bible says in 1 Corinthians 6:19–20, "Do you not know that your body is the temple of the Holy Spirit who is in you, whom you have from God, and you are not your own? For you were bought at a price; therefore glorify God in your body and in your spirit, which are God's." Any sin against the mind, soul, and body is a sin against God, for He created us, and we are the work of His hands.

The Romans, before the fall of Rome, were given to three major sins: gluttony, drunkenness, and immorality. They dug their graves with their teeth, killed themselves by illicit indulgence, and embalmed themselves with alcohol. It is said that at their sumptuous banquets it was a common sight for men to rush to the windows, eject the contents of their stomachs, and then return to the banquet table for further surfeiting. No individual, nor nation, which is given to surfeiting, drunkenness, and gluttony can expect the smile and blessing of God. Millions with excessive appetites and greedy souls, like a dumb animal in new clover, can cast aside all reason and propriety and eat until they die. We read in 1 Timothy 5:6 that "she who lives in pleasure is dead while she lives." Unbalanced living, leaving God out of the picture, inevitably leads to spiritual suicide.

The fact that in an era of record prosperity doctors, counselors, and ministers are working night and day in a frantic effort to relieve the mentally and spiritually distressed proves that we have attained economic prosperity but are starving ourselves spiritually. We have undoubtedly prospered materially, but out of all proportion to our soul development.

Two sides of our nature cry for attention. The body demands food, water, and air, and there is nothing sinful about our satisfying its demands. However, when we cater to the appetites of the flesh to the exclusion and neglect of our souls, we become guilty of the sin of gluttony.

The prodigal son is a classic example of this common human error. He fell prey to materialism. The end result of godless materialism is found in the words: "And when he had spent all, there arose a severe famine in the land, and he began to be in want" (Luke 15:14). Materialism spends itself—so does gluttony, pride, and impurity. They never satisfy because they are slanted toward only one aspect of our nature. The soul can only find sustenance and rest in God.

The thieves on either side of Christ at Calvary represented all that is sinful and loathsome in humanity. They had lived selfishly, greedily, and murderously. But one of them, repentant and broken, had the faith to turn to Jesus and confess Him as Lord. "Then he said to Jesus, 'Lord, remember me'" (Luke 23:42). Christ, ever ready to save, even during the sublime act of redemption, turned and assured him, saying, "Today you will be with Me in Paradise" (Luke 23:43).

When we cater to the *appetites* of the flesh to the exclusion and neglect of our SOULS, we become guilty of the sin of *gluttony*.

GLUTTONY

There are thousands who have lived selfishly and godlessly and are wondering what they can do to undo the past and change the future course of their lives. They can come by repentance of sin and faith to the cross and receive Christ as their Lord and Savior. He will forgive the past and give the power of self-discipline, temperance, and restraint in the days ahead.

A woman called me on the phone during one of our crusades and said, "I have a sin that haunts me day and night. I cannot get victory, and yet I've tried a thousand times. I'm guilty of the sin of gluttony." This was the first time that I had ever had anyone come to me and confess that they were guilty of this sin. I have had many people laughingly tell me that they have "overstuffed," but few consider it a sin. Yet the Bible is specific in stating that gluttony is one of the worst of all sins, and the church has said that it is one of the seven deadly sins.

This woman came to the cross and found forgiveness of the past and victory over gluttony. You, too, can receive Christ, and He will transform your life and give you a power that is beyond yourself to help you to overcome the sins of intemperance, gluttony, and surfeiting. He can give you complete and abiding victory.

Laziness

*"In all labor there is profit, but idle
chatter leads only to poverty"*
(PROVERBS 14:23).

Some Bible teachers suggest that the sin of laziness is not so much a sin of the present era in which we live as it was in the ancient world. However, as I studied my Bible for this message, I became convinced that it is one of the great sins that is being committed.

Webster's dictionary defines *lazy* as "disinclined to activity or exertion; sluggish, slothful, idleness, and indolence."

In theological language it carries with it the idea of not only laziness in physical things, but apathy and inactivity in the practice of our Christianity.

The Bible has a great deal to say about the blighting,

deadening, damning sin of laziness. It says in Proverbs 19:15, "Laziness casts one into a deep sleep, and an idle person will suffer hunger." Again, the Bible says in Proverbs 21:25, "The desire of the lazy man kills him, for his hands refuse to labor."

The Bible indicates that the sin of laziness engenders a negative kind of life that is stagnant and ineffective, and that renders a person unworthy of being a follower of Jesus Christ. Spiritual laziness is not only a sin against God—it is a sin against yourself. It measures the distance between what you ought to be and what you actually are. It shows the difference between the person you are and the person you could be.

Laziness is the destroyer of opportunity and the murderer of souls. It kills stealthily and silently, but it kills just the same.

The lazy person is like driftwood floating downward with the current—effortlessly and heedlessly. The easy way is the popular way, the broad way, the way of the crowd. It takes no effort and no strength to be lost. A drifting boat always goes downstream—never up. A drifting, lazy soul inevitably is drifting toward an eternity of destruction.

Many a person has lost his or her life in an automobile accident, not because this individual was a bad driver, but because he or she was asleep at the wheel.

A *drifting*, lazy soul inevitably is drifting toward an ETERNITY of destruction.

Many individuals are fighting losing battles spiritually, not because they are bad, but because they are spiritually slothful, sleepy, and drowsy. Ephesians 5:14 declares, "Awake, you who sleep, arise from the dead, and Christ will give you light."

Many persons have lost their health and their life, not because they have abused their bodies by sin, but because they have neglected their bodies. They were just too lazy or even too busy to take care of themselves.

Laziness reaps its annual harvest of thousands of deaths, thousands of physical breakdowns, and a staggering amount of suffering and misery across the world.

The sin of doing nothing has been called in the Scriptures the sin of omission—which is just as dangerous as the sin of commission. You do not have to do anything to be lost—just be lazy about your soul, just do nothing. Jesus said that it is easy to be lost. He said, "Wide is the gate and broad is the way that leads to destruction, and there are many who go in by it" (Matthew 7:13).

In the parable of the talents given by Jesus, we read not only of the reward of the faithful servant but of the judgment of the lazy servant. His judgment for doing nothing was as great as the judgment of those that had committed adultery and murder. Matthew 25 records His sentence: "You wicked and lazy servant. . . . Take the talent from him. . . . And cast the unprofitable servant into the outer darkness. There will be weeping and gnashing of teeth" (vv. 26, 28, 30). The unprofitable servant had done no outward wrong—he simply was too lazy to carry out the responsibility that had been assigned to him. His sin was the sin of laziness, the sin of doing nothing.

The chief sin of the ten virgins was not immorality, lying, or cheating—it was laziness. They simply neglected to provide themselves with oil. They were judged not for flagrant sin but for laziness and unfaithfulness. When the bridegroom came, the door of opportunity slammed shut, and the voice of God echoed in judgment, "I do not know you" (Matthew 25:12).

In every area of life, the lazy person loses. The lazy student who spends too much time watching television can never hope to be on the honor roll. Diplomas are usually awarded for faithful work and diligent study—not for native talent or ability. It is usually the person who is willing to work who wins the applause of his or her professors. On the farm, in business, in the school, in the shop, and in every area of our lives, laziness is judged, and faithfulness is rewarded.

Laziness is a destroyer in everyday life. On its account, lives have been lost, cities have been ravaged by fire, and homes have been broken. It has kept someone from a life of respectability, an individual from living a life of purity, and a person from being honest.

Someone has aptly said, "It isn't the thing you do, friend, but the thing you leave undone, that gives you a bit of a heartache at the setting of the sun."

The encouraging word we might have spoken to a discouraged friend, the helpful deed that would have made someone's burden a little lighter, the bit of money pressed lovingly into the hand of the needy—these are the neglected things that bring remorse and rob others of the help they need. When through laziness we fail to do that loving deed, Jesus' words of judgment ring in our ears: "Inasmuch as you did not do it to one of the least of these, you did not do it to Me" (Matthew 25:45).

There are thousands of people who are lazy about going to church. They like to sleep late on Sunday morning or go out for a game of sport. Others like to sit at home and read and rationalize that they can hear a sermon on the radio or watch a religious program on television. They think by thus doing that they have discharged their religious responsibility.

There are others who are lazy about their prayer life. Paul said that we are to "pray without ceasing" (1 Thessalonians 5:17). He meant that we were to always be in the attitude of prayer. Because we are lazy, our

LAZINESS

prayer life is neglected, and thus our spiritual resources are dried up.

I have found that if I leave in the morning without spending a period of time in prayer, the day is completely wrong and troubles and problems mount.

Most of us would rather have that extra wink of sleep than spend fifteen minutes in prayer with God in the morning. We allow everything else to interfere with our appointment with God. If you had an appointment to see the president of the United States or the king of Great Britain at a certain hour, I daresay you would not be tardy or late. You would probably be ahead of time and deeply concerned about how you were dressed, and what you would say to so distinguished a person. Yet we are continually late and tardy in our daily appointment with God. We never prepare our minds for the period of prayer. We usually give God the odd moment or the last moment before we retire, when we are so sleepy that we cannot keep our minds on what we are doing. We are guilty of the sin of laziness.

There are thousands of Christians who are guilty of laziness in Bible reading. First Peter 2:2 teaches that we are to "desire the pure milk of the word, that you may grow thereby." The reason many Christians are not growing is that they are not reading the Bible, and the reason they are not reading the Bible is that they are too lazy. The psalmist said that he meditated in the laws of God both day and night; as a result, God's words were like honeycomb to his heart and soul. Many of us are wondering why we do not have the thrill and joy of Christian experience that we know others have. It is because we are not reading the Bible. We are guilty of the terrible sin of laziness. We are leaving undone those things we ought to have done.

There are many others that are lazy about witnessing for Christ. How long has it been since you spoke to a soul about Christ? How long has it been since you won another person to a saving knowledge of Jesus Christ? There are scores of people that you contact every day that need the Savior, and yet not one word has ever escaped your lips trying to win them to know Christ. You are guilty of the sin of laziness, and others will be lost because you are guilty of this sin.

There are others who are lazy in the way they live. It is a sin to be lazy in dress and in conversation. It is sinful to be lazy in the ordinary courtesies of everyday living.

The sin of laziness extends into many areas, such as: being lazy about driving habits on the highway, thus endangering the lives of others; being lazy about helping those that are in need in our neighborhood; being lazy about giving to charity, so that the unfortunate and the underprivileged do not have the necessities of life.

There are others that are lazy in giving of their tithes and offerings to the kingdom of God. If the average business kept books the way the average Christian keeps books in relation to his or her debts and gifts to God, it would go bankrupt within a few days.

There are thousands of Christians who are slumbering and keeping their mouths shut while the world is in desperate need of the gospel of Jesus Christ. The Bible warns in Isaiah 56:10 that "his watchmen are blind, they are all ignorant; they are all dumb dogs, they cannot bark; sleeping, lying down, loving to slumber." Romans 12:11 advises us to be "not lagging in diligence, fervent in spirit, serving the Lord." There are many ways that you can serve Christ, no matter what your circumstances.

The New Testament continually warns against the sin of laziness: "That you do not become sluggish, but imitate those who through faith and patience inherit the promises" (Hebrews 6:12). Martin Luther wrote in one of his sermons:

> The Devil held a great anniversary at which his emissaries were convened to report the results of their several missions.
>
> "I let loose the wild beasts of the desert," said one, "on a caravan of Christians; and their bones are now bleaching in the sands."

"What of that?" said the Devil. "Their souls were all saved."

"I drove the east wind," said another, "against a ship freighted with Christians, and they were all drowned."

"What of that?" said the Devil. "Their souls were saved."

"For ten years I tried to get a person to be at ease about his soul, and at last I succeeded, and he is ours," said another.

Then the Devil shouted, and the night stars of hell sang for joy.

The sin of laziness and criminal spiritual neglect has probably done as much to populate hell as the vicious sins we hear so much about. It seems so harmless, so innocent, and yet its venom is more deadly to the spirit of humans than some of the most hideous sins to which we are addicted.

The worst thing that laziness does is to rob a person of spiritual purpose—the power of Christian decision. In stupidity and indolence, this spiritual laziness renders the person incapable of choosing Christ. An individual may give mental assent to the truth—he or she may even know the doctrines of religion—but this person is incapable of

The worst thing that *laziness* does is to rob a person of spiritual purpose—the POWER of Christian decision. In stupidity and indolence, this SPIRITUAL laziness renders the person incapable of choosing *Christ*.

positive action. The road is clear; this individual knows the way he or she should go, but laziness has made his or her will soft and irresponsible. This sin must be confessed like any other. James 4:17 says, "To him who knows to do good and does not do it, to him it is sin."

In the crowd of people who gathered around the cross of Christ were those who were committing the sin of laziness. Even though Christ, the Son of God, was dying, people were "sitting down, keeping watch over Him there" (Matthew 27:36). Such indifference! Such unthinkable laziness! But just before Jesus breathed His last breath, He looked at the sinners all around Him—the thieves, the murderers, the gamblers, the hypocrites, the profane, the immoral, the proud, the envious, the greedy, the gluttonous, and the lazy—and He said, "Father, forgive them, for they do not know what they do" (Luke 23:34). In that moment, the Lamb of God (to everyone who would believe) took away the sins of the world. By that redemptive, consummate act, He opened up the way to heaven.

Eternal life is within reach of everyone. The Savior is as near as your yielded will, or He is as far away as you want Him to be. Your own stubborn, lazy spirit is your greatest hindrance to letting Him come into your heart.

Greed

*"He who loves silver will not be satisfied
with silver; nor he who loves abundance,
with increase. This also is vanity."*

ECCLESIASTES 5:10

Greed, the close relative of covetousness, is probably the parent of more evil than all the other sins. In fact, 1 Timothy 6:10 says that the "love of money is a root of all kinds of evil." Individuals driven by greed have robbed, assaulted, attacked, embezzled, slandered, and murdered. Covetousness was one of the first sins to raise its venomous head in the garden of Eden. In Genesis 3:6 we read that "when the woman saw that the tree was good for food, and it was pleasant to the eyes, and a tree desirable to make one wise, she took of its fruit and ate."

This sin of greed is as much a part of the natural person as breathing. From babyhood to old age, it motivates our actions and shapes our behavior patterns. It has also forced its way into our ethical ideology. Such catchphrases as "self-preservation is man's first instinct," "self-protection is the first law of life," "look out for number one" are all adages of greed.

The garden of Eden was a place of indescribable beauty until the sin of greed crept in. After that it was an eerie swamp with a flaming sword of judgment that turned every way. Life can never be hallowed with the bliss of Eden, and people can never know the fellowship of God until he or she finds victory over the blighting sin of greed and selfishness. No sin can rob life of its beauty and radiance as thoroughly as the sin of greed.

Scan through the pages of the Bible and note the trail of abject misery that this deadly sin has made through human history. It was an unholy, unnatural lust for selfish gain that caused King Ahab to covet Naboth's vineyard and eventually to murder to achieve his avaricious end. But the voice of God came to Ahab, saying, "In the place where dogs licked the blood of Naboth, dogs shall lick your blood" (1 Kings 21:19).

Greed first claims our souls, then seals our destiny.

Greed first claims our SOULS, then seals our *destiny*.

Ahab little dreamed that the innocent seed of greed in his heart would in the end bring forth a harvest of death and judgment. Joseph's brothers sowed the tiny seed of greed when they sold their godly brother into slavery, but little did they foresee the harvest of famine and misery that they were to reap when greed came into full bloom.

The rich man of whom Jesus spoke sowed a crop of selfishness and greed, and Jesus said that it brought forth plentifully. This rich man soon came to know the futility that comes from full barns, full pockets, but an empty heart. The rich man soon dropped dead as a voice from heaven said, "Fool! This night your soul will be required of you" (Luke 12:20).

Judas, driven by greed, sold his Lord for thirty pieces of silver but found out that life was not worth living without Him. Throwing the tarnished silver at the feet of the greedy men with whom he had made a poor bargain, Judas went out and hanged himself; but long before the life was choked out of the body, his soul was dead—it had been strangled by greed. To all the Ahabs, the Judases, the foolish men of every age who live selfishly and greedily, Christ says in Luke 12:21, "So is he who lays up treasures for himself, and is not rich toward God."

Greed seeks more than its own in life. It cheats, robs, murders, and slanders to achieve its desires. The Bible teaches that we are born with the sin of greed. We read in Jeremiah 6:13 that "from the least of them even to the greatest of them, everyone is given to covetousness." Babies are born with selfish, grasping, greedy natures. Though they cannot make requirements known in words, they have a way of making their desires known.

I was in a home once where the parents and grandparents were running in every direction in a frantic effort to gratify the desires of a single baby. Even growing children are selfish by nature. "Daddy, what did you get me?" was as familiar a cry in my home as it might be in yours.

As long as the prodigal son sang the song of "Give me," his lot was misery, want, loneliness, and famine; but when he changed his song to "Forgive me," he found himself in a state of fellowship, comfort, and plenty.

Nineteenth-century theologian Charles Kingsley said,

> If you want to be miserable yourself, and a maker of misery to others, the way is easy enough. Only be selfish, and it is done at once. Be defiled and unbelieving. Defile and foul God's good gifts by self, and by loving yourself more than what is right. Do not believe that the good God knows your needs before you ask and will give you whatsoever is good for you. Think about yourself; about what *you* want, what *you* like, what

respect people ought to pay *you*, what people think of *you*: and then to you nothing will be pure. You will spoil everything you touch; you will make sin and misery for yourself out of everything which God sends you; you will be as wretched as you choose on earth.[1]

Covetousness has been rated in Romans 1:29 with the more open and vicious sins: "Being filled with all unrighteousness, sexual immorality, wickedness, covetousness, maliciousness." In Romans 13:9 it is mentioned with murder, immorality, stealing, and lying. This sin, which has stunted the spiritual development of so many people and has appeared so harmless, is considered in the Word of God as one of the most hideous and destructive of all Satan's tools. In fact, the Bible goes so far as to warn that a covetous and greedy person cannot inherit the kingdom of God (1 Corinthians 6:10).

The Bible teaches that greed is idolatry. A piece of silver can be held so close to your eyes that you cannot see the sun, and the love of money can so fill your heart that God will be crowded out. In this age of materialism, the consuming passion for material gain has made millions forget the words of Jesus in Mark 8:36: "What will it profit a man if he gains the whole world and loses his own soul?" If our lives are to show a profit when our record books are balanced, there must be more than dollar signs written there.

The love of money corrodes the hearts of men, spoiling their happiness and setting them in conflict with one another. The lust of one country for the soil of another has thousands of times let loose war and pillage on innocent populations. The powerful have, in every age, under the sway of similar motives, plundered the goods and oppressed the persons of the weak. Employers down through the centuries have extracted the toll from laborers, even while their consciences told them that they were not paying wages commensurate with the work being done.

It was the sin of greed that caused slavery and the suffering, misery, and death that accompanied this plague of humanity. The love of money is what causes the robberies that we read about and often causes murder. It is the sin of greed that causes a lawyer to lie and an operator on the stock market to swindle his clients.

Horace is credited for saying, "Isne tibi melius suadet, qui 'rem facias, rem, si possis, recte, si non, quocumque modo rem," which translates from Latin to English as, "Is he to you better he who persuades, make money, money, if possible, uprightly, if not, by any means money."[2]

The great sin of America is greed and covetousness.

The great sin of America is *greed* and covetousness. We are so bent on making MONEY that we do not have time for God and *spiritual* exercise.

GREED

We are so bent on making money that we do not have time for God and spiritual exercise. Many businesses are kept open unnecessarily on Sunday and religious holidays, thus desecrating God's day in order to gain a few extra dollars. People are so busy making money they have no time for God. Individuals do not realize that in their desire for ease, luxury, and the making of money, they may soon lose all in the most horrifying and terrible destruction the world has ever known. I beg of you, wake up before it's too late!

It is the sin of greed that causes gamblers to have fever in their blood and drives them on, recklessly hardening their hearts until they have lost not only their money but their souls.

Some time ago a party of tourists traveling through Death Valley, California, discovered the skeleton of a man who had died on the drifting dunes of the desert. Clutched in his bony hand was a chunk of mica whose pyrites, resembling gold, had deceived him. He had mistaken the yellow streaks in this rock for gold. On a scrap of paper under the skeleton were written the words, "Died rich." He had thought he was rich, but starved to death, lost and alone. Such is the deceitfulness of riches. If we have nothing more than money, we are poor indeed.

There are many people who think they are rich in

economic security, but they are actually poor toward God. One of the saddest pictures in the New Testament is that of the rich young ruler leaving Jesus sorrowfully, with his pockets full but his heart empty. He was interested in eternal life, but he wasn't willing to pay the price. That is true in the lives of many today. Many, like this rich youth, know the way—but they are not willing to pay the price.

It is not a sin to be rich. If you have gotten your riches honestly, then God considers you a steward of that which He has given you. But if your riches have choked out your spiritual life, then it has become sin—and you are poverty-stricken in God's sight. We read about several rich men in the Bible who were righteous and godly men, who dedicated their riches to God.

Almost every individual is considered a rich person if they have shoes to wear, clothes on their back, and food to eat. So, the sin of greed is actually one of the great sins, and probably the greatest stumbling block to the kingdom of heaven today.

There are many people who say that the sin of greed is incurable and that once a person is being choked by this sin there is no salvation. I grant you that Jesus warned that it is easier for a camel to go through the eye of a needle than it is for a person who trusts in riches to get to heaven (Matthew 19:24); yet it is possible for a person

GREED

who is guilty of this sin to be saved. You may be a poor person, but greed and lust for money have hardened your heart and made you bitter and envious. It is possible for even you to be saved. You may come in repentance of your sin and faith in the Lord Jesus Christ, and His blood can cleanse from every sin. You can find wonderful, glorious, and blessed forgiveness at the foot of the cross—no matter what your sin.

Praying the Scriptures

PRIDE

"The wicked in his proud countenance does not seek God; God is in none of his thoughts." **Psalm 10:4**

"For You will save the humble people, but will bring down haughty looks." **Psalm 18:27**

"The humble He guides in justice, and the humble He teaches His way." **Psalm 25:9**

"Though the Lord is on high, yet He regards the lowly; but the proud He knows from afar." **Psalm 138:6**

"Surely He scorns the scornful, but gives grace to the humble." **Proverbs 3:34**

"The fear of the LORD is to hate evil; pride and arrogance and the evil way and the perverse mouth I hate." **Proverbs 8:13**

"The fear of the LORD is the instruction of wisdom, and before honor is humility." **Proverbs 15:33**

"Before destruction the heart of a man is haughty, and before honor is humility." **Proverbs 18:12**

"By humility and the fear of the LORD are riches and honor and life." **Proverbs 22:4**

"The lofty looks of man shall be humbled, the haughtiness of men shall be bowed down, and the LORD alone shall be exalted in that day." **Isaiah 2:11**

"The LORD of hosts has purposed it, to bring to dishonor the pride of all glory, to bring into contempt all the honorable of the earth." **Isaiah 23:9**

"For thus says the High and Lofty One who inhabits eternity, whose name is Holy: 'I dwell in the high and holy place, with him who has a contrite and humble spirit, to revive the spirit of the humble, and to revive the heart of the contrite ones.'" **Isaiah 57:15**

"Now I, Nebuchadnezzar, praise and extol and honor the King of heaven, all of whose works are truth, and His ways justice. And those who walk in pride He is able to put down." **Daniel 4:37**

"The pride of your heart has deceived you, you who dwell in the clefts of the rock, whose habitation is high; you who say in your heart, 'Who will bring me down to the ground?'" **Obadiah 1:3**

"In that day you shall not be ashamed for any of your deeds in which you transgressed against Me; for then I will take away from your midst those who rejoice in your pride, and you shall no longer be haughty in My holy mountain." **Zephaniah 3:11**

"Blessed are the poor in spirit, for theirs is the kingdom of heaven." **Matthew 5:3**

"And whoever exalts himself will be humbled, and he who humbles himself will be exalted." **Matthew 23:12**

"I tell you, this man went down to his house justified rather than the other; for everyone who exalts himself will be humbled, and he who humbles himself will be exalted." **Luke 18:14**

"For I say, through the grace given to me, to everyone who is among you, not to think of himself more highly than he ought to think, but to think soberly, as God has dealt to each one a measure of faith." **Romans 12:3**

"Be of the same mind toward one another. Do not set your mind on high things, but associate with the humble. Do not be wise in your own opinion." **Romans 12:16**

"Therefore let him who thinks he stands take heed lest he fall." **1 Corinthians 10:12**

"Let nothing be done through selfish ambition or conceit, but in lowliness of mind let each esteem others better than himself." **Philippians 2:3**

"Humble yourselves in the sight of the Lord, and He will lift you up." **James 4:10**

"Likewise you younger people, submit yourselves to your elders. Yes, all of you be submissive to one another, and be clothed with humility, for 'God resists the proud, but gives grace to the humble.' Therefore humble yourselves under the mighty hand of God, that He may exalt you in due time." **1 Peter 5:5-6**

"For all that is in the world—the lust of the flesh, the lust of the eyes, and the pride of life—is not of the Father but is of the world." **1 John 2:16**

ANGER

"The LORD is merciful and gracious, slow to anger, and abounding in mercy." **Psalm 103:8**

"The LORD is gracious and full of compassion, slow to anger and great in mercy." **Psalm 145:8**

"A soft answer turns away wrath, but a harsh word stirs up anger." **Proverbs 15:1**

"A wrathful man stirs up strife, but he who is slow to anger allays contention." **Proverbs 15:18**

"The beginning of strife is like releasing water; therefore stop contention before a quarrel starts." **Proverbs 17:14**

"The discretion of a man makes him slow to anger, and his glory is to overlook a transgression." **Proverbs 19:11**

"Make no friendship with an angry man, and with a furious man do not go, lest you learn his ways and set a snare for your soul." **Proverbs 22:24–25**

"An angry man stirs up strife, and a furious man abounds in transgression." **Proverbs 29:22**

"Do not hasten in your spirit to be angry, for anger rests in the bosom of fools." **Ecclesiastes 7:9**

"But I say to you, love your enemies, bless those who curse you, do good to those who hate you, and pray for those who spitefully use you and persecute you." **Matthew 5:44**

"Take My yoke upon you and learn from Me, for I am gentle and lowly in heart, and you will find rest for your souls." **Matthew 11:29**

"But those things which proceed out of the mouth come from the heart, and they defile a man." **Matthew 15:18**

"But I say to you who hear: Love your enemies, do good to those who hate you, bless those who curse you, and pray for those who spitefully use you." **Luke 6:27–28**

"For I see that you are poisoned by bitterness and bound by iniquity." **Acts 8:23**

"Beloved, do not avenge yourselves, but rather give place to wrath; for it is written, 'Vengeance is Mine, I will repay,' says the Lord." **Romans 12:19**

"Do not be overcome by evil, but overcome evil with good." **Romans 12:21**

"'Be angry, and do not sin': do not let the sun go down on your wrath, nor give place to the devil." **Ephesians 4:26–27**

"Let all bitterness, wrath, anger, clamor, and evil speaking be put away from you, with all malice. And be kind to one another, tenderhearted, forgiving one another, even as God in Christ forgave you." **Ephesians 4:31–32**

"Let this mind be in you which was also in Christ Jesus." **Philippians 2:5**

"Therefore, as the elect of God, holy and beloved, put on tender mercies, kindness, humility, meekness, longsuffering; bearing with one another, and forgiving one another, if anyone has a complaint against another; even as Christ forgave you, so you also must do." **Colossians 3:12–13**

"Pursue peace with all people, and holiness, without which no one will see the Lord: looking carefully lest anyone fall short of the grace of God; lest any root of bitterness springing up cause trouble, and by this many become defiled." **Hebrews 12:14–15**

"Where do wars and fights come from among you? Do they not come from your desires for pleasure that war in your members? You lust and do not have. You murder and covet and cannot obtain. You fight and war." **James 4:1–2**

"Therefore, laying aside all malice, all deceit, hypocrisy, envy, and all evil speaking, as newborn babes, desire the pure milk of the word, that you may grow thereby, if indeed you have tasted that the Lord is gracious." **1 Peter 2:1–4**

"Not returning evil for evil or reviling for reviling, but on the contrary blessing, knowing that you were called to this, that you may inherit a blessing." **1 Peter 3:9**

"If someone says, 'I love God,' and hates his brother, he is a liar; for he who does not love his brother whom he has seen, how can he love God whom he has not seen?" **1 John 4:20**

ENVY

"Do not fret because of evildoers, nor be envious of the workers of iniquity. For they shall soon be cut down like the grass, and wither as the green herb." **Psalm 37:1–2**

"Rest in the LORD, and wait patiently for Him; do not fret because of him who prospers in his way, because of the man who brings wicked schemes to pass." **Psalm 37:7**

"Incline my heart to Your testimonies, and not to covetousness." **Psalm 119:36**

"Do not envy the oppressor, and choose none of his ways." **Proverbs 3:31**

"For jealousy is a husband's fury; therefore he will not spare in the day of vengeance." **Proverbs 6:34**

"The foolishness of a man twists his way, and his heart frets against the LORD." **Proverbs 19:3**

"Do not let your heart envy sinners, but be zealous for the fear of the LORD all the day." **Proverbs 23:17**

"Do not be envious of evil men, nor desire to be with them; for their heart devises violence, and their lips talk of troublemaking." **Proverbs 24:1–2**

"Do not fret because of evildoers, nor be envious of the wicked; for there will be no prospect for the evil man; the lamp of the wicked will be put out." **Proverbs 24:19–20**

"Again, I saw that for all toil and every skillful work a man is envied by his neighbor. This also is vanity and grasping for the wind." **Ecclesiastes 4:4**

"Therefore do not worry about tomorrow, for tomorrow will worry about its own things. Sufficient for the day is its own trouble." **Matthew 6:34**

"Is it not lawful for me to do what I wish with my own things? Or is your eye evil because I am good?" **Matthew 20:15**

"For he knew that they had handed Him over because of envy." **Matthew 27:18**

"And the patriarchs, becoming envious, sold Joseph into Egypt. But God was with him." **Acts 7:9**

"Being filled with all unrighteousness, sexual immorality, wickedness, covetousness, maliciousness; full of envy, murder, strife, deceit, evil-mindedness; they are whisperers." **Romans 1:29**

"Let us walk properly, as in the day, not in revelry and drunkenness, not in lewdness and lust, not in strife and envy." **Romans 13:13**

"For you are still carnal. For where there are envy, strife, and divisions among you, are you not carnal and behaving like mere men?" **1 Corinthians 3:3**

"Love suffers long and is kind; love does not envy; love does not parade itself, is not puffed up." **1 Corinthians 13:4**

"[Love] does not behave rudely, does not seek its own, is not provoked, thinks no evil." **1 Corinthians 13:5**

"Let nothing be done through selfish ambition or conceit, but in lowliness of mind let each esteem others better than himself." **Philippians 2:3**

"Now godliness with contentment is great gain." **1 Timothy 6:6**

"For we ourselves were also once foolish, disobedient, deceived, serving various lusts and pleasures, living in malice and envy, hateful and hating one another." **Titus 3:3**

"Let your conduct be without covetousness; be content with such things as you have. For He Himself has said, 'I will never leave you nor forsake you.'" **Hebrews 13:5**

"Do not grumble against one another, brethren, lest you be condemned. Behold, the Judge is standing at the door!" **James 5:9**

"Therefore, laying aside all malice, all deceit, hypocrisy, envy, and all evil speaking." **1 Peter 2:1**

"For where envy and self-seeking exist, confusion and every evil thing are there." **James 3:16**

IMPURITY

"Who may ascend into the hill of the LORD? Or who may stand in His holy place? He who has clean hands and a pure heart, who has not lifted up his soul to an idol, nor sworn deceitfully." **Psalm 24:3–4**

"How can a young man cleanse his way? By taking heed according to Your word." **Psalm 119:9**

"Blessed are the pure in heart, for they shall see God." **Matthew 5:8**

"Not everyone who says to Me, 'Lord, Lord,' shall enter the kingdom of heaven, but he who does the will of My Father in heaven. Many will say to Me in that day, 'Lord, Lord, have we not prophesied in Your name, cast out demons in Your name, and done many wonders in Your name?' And then I will declare to them, 'I never knew you; depart from Me, you who practice lawlessness!'" **Matthew 7:21–23**

"But those things which proceed out of the mouth come from the heart, and they defile a man. For out of the heart proceed evil thoughts, murders, adulteries, fornications, thefts, false witness, blasphemies." **Matthew 15:18–19**

"Therefore God also gave them up to uncleanness, in the lusts of their hearts, to dishonor their bodies among themselves, who exchanged the truth of God for the lie, and worshiped and served the creature rather than the Creator, who is blessed forever. Amen." **Romans 1:24–25**

"Therefore do not let sin reign in your mortal body, that you should obey it in its lusts. And do not present your members as instruments of unrighteousness to sin, but present yourselves to God as being alive from the dead, and your members as instruments of righteousness to God." **Romans 6:12–13**

"For if you live according to the flesh you will die; but if by the Spirit you put to death the deeds of the body, you will live." **Romans 8:13**

"I beseech you therefore, brethren, by the mercies of God, that you present your bodies a living sacrifice, holy, acceptable to God, which is your reasonable service. And do not be conformed to this world, but be transformed by the renewing of your mind, that you may prove what is that good and acceptable and perfect will of God." **Romans 12:1–2**

"Let us walk properly, as in the day, not in revelry and drunkenness, not in lewdness and lust, not in strife and envy." **Romans 13:13**

"Flee sexual immorality. Every sin that a man does is outside the body, but he who commits sexual immorality sins against his own body. Or do you not know that your body is the temple of the Holy Spirit who is in you, whom you have from God, and you are not your own? For you were bought at a price; therefore glorify God in your body and in your spirit, which are God's." **1 Corinthians 6:18–20**

"Therefore, having these promises, beloved, let us cleanse ourselves from all filthiness of the flesh and spirit, perfecting holiness in the fear of God." **2 Corinthians 7:1**

"That you put off, concerning your former conduct, the old man which grows corrupt according to the deceitful lusts, and be renewed in the spirit of your mind, and that you put on the new man which was created according to God, in true righteousness and holiness." **Ephesians 4:22–24**

"But fornication and all uncleanness or covetousness, let it not even be named among you, as is fitting for saints." **Ephesians 5:3**

"Finally, brethren, whatever things are true, whatever things are noble, whatever things are just, whatever things are pure, whatever things are lovely, whatever things are of good report, if there is any virtue and if there is anything praiseworthy—meditate on these things." **Philippians 4:8**

"Therefore put to death your members which are on the earth: fornication, uncleanness, passion, evil desire, and covetousness, which is idolatry." **Colossians 3:5**

"For this is the will of God, your sanctification: that you should abstain from sexual immorality; that each of you should know how to possess his own vessel in sanctification and honor, not in passion of lust, like the Gentiles who do not know God." **1 Thessalonians 4:3–5**

"Let no one despise your youth, but be an example to the believers in word, in conduct, in love, in spirit, in faith, in purity." **1 Timothy 4:12**

"Flee also youthful lusts; but pursue righteousness, faith, love, peace with those who call on the Lord out of a pure heart." **2 Timothy 2:22**

"For the grace of God that brings salvation has appeared to all men, teaching us that, denying ungodliness and worldly lusts, we should live soberly, righteously, and godly in the present age." **Titus 2:11–12**

"Marriage is honorable among all, and the bed undefiled; but fornicators and adulterers God will judge." **Hebrews 13:4**

"Draw near to God and He will draw near to you. Cleanse your hands, you sinners; and purify your hearts, you double-minded." **James 4:8**

"But as He who called you is holy, you also be holy in all your conduct, because it is written, 'Be holy, for I am holy.'" **1 Peter 1:15–16**

"Do not love the world or the things in the world. If anyone loves the world, the love of the Father is not in him. For all that is in the world—the lust of the flesh, the lust of the eyes, and the pride of life—is not of the Father but is of the world. And the world is passing away, and the lust of it; but he who does the will of God abides forever." **1 John 2:15–17**

"And everyone who has this hope in Him purifies himself, just as He is pure." **1 John 3:3**

GLUTTONY

"And they tested God in their heart by asking for the food of their fancy." **Psalm 78:18**

"And put a knife to your throat if you are a man given to appetite." **Proverbs 23:2**

"It is not good to eat much honey; so to seek one's own glory is not glory." **Proverbs 25:27**

"Whoever has no rule over his own spirit is like a city broken down, without walls." **Proverbs 25:28**

"Whoever keeps the law is a discerning son, but a companion of gluttons shames his father." **Proverbs 28:7**

"Give me neither poverty nor riches—feed me with the food allotted to me; lest I be full and deny You, and say, 'Who is the LORD?' Or lest I be poor and steal, and profane the name of my God." **Proverbs 30:8–9**

"The leech has two daughters—Give and Give! There are three things that are never satisfied, four never say, 'Enough!'" **Proverbs 30:15**

"All the labor of man is for his mouth, and yet the soul is not satisfied." **Ecclesiastes 6:7**

"It is written, 'Man shall not live by bread alone, but by every word that proceeds from the mouth of God.'" **Matthew 4:4**

"Therefore I say to you, do not worry about your life, what you will eat or what you will drink; nor about your body, what you will put on. Is not life more than food and the body more than clothing?" **Matthew 6:25**

"But take heed to yourselves, lest your hearts be weighed down with carousing, drunkenness, and cares of this life, and that Day come on you unexpectedly." **Luke 21:34**

Freedom from the Seven Deadly Sins

"Therefore, brethren, we are debtors—not to the flesh, to live according to the flesh. For if you live according to the flesh you will die; but if by the Spirit you put to death the deeds of the body, you will live." **Romans 8:12–13**

"But put on the Lord Jesus Christ, and make no provision for the flesh, to fulfill its lusts." **Romans 13:14**

"For the kingdom of God is not eating and drinking, but righteousness and peace and joy in the Holy Spirit." **Romans 14:17**

"Do you not know that you are the temple of God and that the Spirit of God dwells in you? If anyone defiles the temple of God, God will destroy him. For the temple of God is holy, which temple you are." **1 Corinthians 3:16–17**

"But I discipline my body and bring it into subjection, lest, when I have preached to others, I myself should become disqualified." **1 Corinthians 9:27**

"Therefore, whether you eat or drink, or whatever you do, do all to the glory of God." **1 Corinthians 10:31**

"Now the works of the flesh are evident, which are: adultery, fornication, uncleanness, lewdness, idolatry, sorcery, hatred, contentions, jealousies, outbursts of wrath, selfish ambitions, dissensions, heresies, envy, murders, drunkenness, revelries, and the like; of which I tell you beforehand, just as I also told you in time past, that those who practice such things will not inherit the kingdom of God." **Galatians 5:19–21**

"Therefore put to death your members which are on the earth: fornication, uncleanness, passion, evil desire, and covetousness, which is idolatry." **Colossians 3:5**

"Forbidding to marry, and commanding to abstain from foods which God created to be received with thanksgiving by those who believe and know the truth. For every creature of God is good, and nothing is to be refused if it is received with thanksgiving; for it is sanctified by the word of God and prayer." **1 Timothy 4:3-5**

"One of them, a prophet of their own, said, 'Cretans are always liars, evil beasts, lazy gluttons.' This testimony is true. Therefore rebuke them sharply, that they may be sound in the faith." **Titus 1:12–13**

"Lest there be any fornicator or profane person like Esau, who for one morsel of food sold his birthright." **Hebrews 12:16**

"But each one is tempted when he is drawn away by his own desires and enticed." **James 1:14**

"And will receive the wages of unrighteousness, as those who count it pleasure to carouse in the daytime. They are spots and blemishes, carousing in their own deceptions while they feast with you." **2 Peter 2:13**

"For all that is in the world—the lust of the flesh, the lust of the eyes, and the pride of life—is not of the Father but is of the world." **1 John 2:16**

LAZINESS

"Then the Lord God took the man and put him in the garden of Eden to tend and keep it." **Genesis 2:15**

"Go to the ant, you sluggard! Consider her ways and be wise, which, having no captain, overseer or ruler, provides her supplies in the summer, and gathers her food in the harvest." **Proverbs 6:6-8**

"He who has a slack hand becomes poor, but the hand of the diligent makes rich." **Proverbs 10:4**

"He who tills his land will be satisfied with bread, but he who follows frivolity is devoid of understanding." **Proverbs 12:11**

"The hand of the diligent will rule, but the lazy man will be put to forced labor." **Proverbs 12:24**

"The soul of a lazy man desires, and has nothing; but the soul of the diligent shall be made rich." **Proverbs 13:4**

"In all labor there is profit, but idle chatter leads only to poverty." **Proverbs 14:23**

"The way of the lazy man is like a hedge of thorns, but the way of the upright is a highway." **Proverbs 15:19**

"The person who labors, labors for himself, for his hungry mouth drives him on." **Proverbs 16:26**

"He who is slothful in his work is a brother to him who is a great destroyer." **Proverbs 18:9**

"The lazy man will not plow because of winter; he will beg during harvest and have nothing." **Proverbs 20:4**

"The lazy man says, 'There is a lion outside! I shall be slain in the streets!'" **Proverbs 22:13**

"I went by the field of the lazy man, and by the vineyard of the man devoid of understanding; and there it was, all overgrown with thorns; its surface was covered with nettles; its stone wall was broken down. When I saw it, I considered it well; I looked on it and received instruction: A little sleep, a little slumber, a little folding of the hands to rest; so shall your poverty come like a prowler, and your need like an armed man." **Proverbs 24:30–34**

"Whatever your hand finds to do, do it with your might; for there is no work or device or knowledge or wisdom in the grave where you are going." **Ecclesiastes 9:10**

"Because of laziness the building decays, and through idleness of hands the house leaks." **Ecclesiastes 10:18**

"Therefore whoever hears these sayings of Mine, and does them, I will liken him to a wise man who built his house on the rock: and the rain descended, the floods came, and the winds blew and beat on that house; and it did not fall, for it was founded on the rock. But everyone who hears these sayings of Mine, and does not do them, will be like a foolish man who built his house on the sand: and the rain descended, the floods came, and the winds blew and beat on that house; and it fell. And great was its fall."
Matthew 7:24–27

"And the Lord said, 'Who then is that faithful and wise steward, whom his master will make ruler over his household, to give them their portion of food in due season? Blessed is that servant whom his master will find so doing when he comes. Truly, I say to you that he will make him ruler over all that he has. But if that servant says in his heart, "My master is delaying his coming," and begins to beat the male and female servants, and to eat and drink and be drunk, the master of that servant will come on a day when he is not looking for him, and at an hour when he is not aware, and will cut him in two and appoint him his portion with the unbelievers.'"
Luke 12:42–46

"Whatever you do in word or deed, do all in the name of the Lord Jesus, giving thanks to God the Father through Him." **Colossians 3:17**

"And whatever you do, do it heartily, as to the Lord and not to men, knowing that from the Lord you will receive the reward of the inheritance; for you serve the Lord Christ." **Colossians 3:23–24**

"That you also aspire to lead a quiet life, to mind your own business, and to work with your own hands, as we commanded you, that you may walk properly toward those who are outside, and that you may lack nothing." **1 Thessalonians 4:11–12**

"For even when we were with you, we commanded you this: If anyone will not work, neither shall he eat." **2 Thessalonians 3:10**

"But if anyone does not provide for his own, and especially for those of his household, he has denied the faith and is worse than an unbeliever." **1 Timothy 5:8**

"For the grace of God that brings salvation has appeared to all men, teaching us that, denying ungodliness and worldly lusts, we should live soberly, righteously, and godly in the present age." **Titus 2:11–12**

"And let us consider one another in order to stir up love and good works, not forsaking the assembling of ourselves together, as is the manner of some, but exhorting one another, and so much the more as you see the Day approaching." **Hebrews 10:24–25**

"For as the body without the spirit is dead, so faith without works is dead also." **James 2:26**

GREED

"So are the ways of everyone who is greedy for gain; it takes away the life of its owners." **Proverbs 1:19**

"He who trusts in his riches will fall, but the righteous will flourish like foliage." **Proverbs 11:28**

"He who is greedy for gain troubles his own house, but he who hates bribes will live." **Proverbs 15:27**

"Do not overwork to be rich; because of your own understanding, cease! Will you set your eyes on that which is not? For riches certainly make themselves wings; they fly away like an eagle toward heaven." **Proverbs 23:4–5**

"He who is of a proud heart stirs up strife, but he who trusts in the Lord will be prospered." **Proverbs 28:25**

"He who loves silver will not be satisfied with silver; nor he who loves abundance, with increase. This also is vanity." **Ecclesiastes 5:10**

"Do not lay up for yourselves treasures on earth, where moth and rust destroy and where thieves break in and steal; but lay up for yourselves treasures in heaven, where neither moth nor rust destroys and where thieves do not break in and steal. For where your treasure is, there your heart will be also." **Matthew 6:19–21**

"No one can serve two masters; for either he will hate the one and love the other, or else he will be loyal to the one and despise the other. You cannot serve God and mammon." **Matthew 6:24**

"And again I say to you, it is easier for a camel to go through the eye of a needle than for a rich man to enter the kingdom of God." **Matthew 19:24**

"For from within, out of the heart of men, proceed evil thoughts, adulteries, fornications, murders, thefts, covetousness, wickedness, deceit, lewdness, an evil eye, blasphemy, pride, foolishness. All these evil things come from within and defile a man." **Mark 7:21–23**

"For what will it profit a man if he gains the whole world, and loses his own soul? Or what will a man give in exchange for his soul?" **Mark 8:36–37**

"And He said to them, 'Take heed and beware of covetousness, for one's life does not consist in the abundance of the things he possesses.'" **Luke 12:15**

"Then He spoke a parable to them, saying: 'The ground of a certain rich man yielded plentifully. And he thought within himself, saying, "What shall I do, since I have no room to store my crops?" So he said, "I will do this: I will pull down my barns and build greater, and there I will store all my crops and my goods. And I will say to my soul, "Soul, you have many goods laid up for many years; take your ease; eat, drink, and be merry." But God said to him, "Fool! This night your soul will be required of you; then whose will those things be which you have provided?" So is he who lays up treasure for himself, and is not rich toward God.'" **Luke 12:16–21**

"No servant can serve two masters; for either he will hate the one and love the other, or else he will be loyal to the one and despise the other. You cannot serve God and mammon." **Luke 16:13**

"I have coveted no one's silver or gold or apparel. Yes, you yourselves know that these hands have provided for my necessities, and for those who were with me. I have shown you in every way, by laboring like this, that you must support the weak. And remember the words of the Lord Jesus, that He said, 'It is more blessed to give than to receive.'" **Acts 20:33–35**

"For the commandments, 'You shall not commit adultery,' 'You shall not murder,' 'You shall not steal,' 'You shall not bear false witness against your neighbor,' and 'You shall not covet' are all summed up in this saying, namely, 'You shall love your neighbor as yourself.'" **Romans 13:9**

"So let each one give as he purposes in his heart, not grudgingly or of necessity; for God loves a cheerful giver." **2 Corinthians 9:7**

"For this you know, that no fornicator, unclean person, nor covetous man, who is an idolater, has any inheritance in the kingdom of Christ and God." **Ephesians 5:5**

"Therefore put to death your members which are on the earth: fornication, uncleanness, passion, evil desire, and covetousness, which is idolatry." **Colossians 3:5**

"Now godliness with contentment is great gain. For we brought nothing into this world, and it is certain we can carry nothing out. And having food and clothing, with these we shall be content. But those who desire to be rich fall into temptation and a snare, and into many foolish and harmful lusts which drown men in destruction and perdition. For the love of money is a root of all kinds of evil, for which some have strayed from the faith in their greediness, and pierced themselves through with many sorrows." **1 Timothy 6:6–10**

"Command those who are rich in this present age not to be haughty, nor to trust in uncertain riches but in the living God, who gives us richly all things to enjoy. Let them do good, that they be rich in good works, ready to give, willing to share, storing up for themselves a good foundation for the time to come, that they may lay hold on eternal life." **1 Timothy 6:17–19**

"Let your conduct be without covetousness; be content with such things as you have. For He Himself has said, 'I will never leave you nor forsake you.'" **Hebrews 13:5**

"Come now, you rich, weep and howl for your miseries that are coming upon you! Your riches are corrupted, and your garments are moth-eaten. Your gold and silver are corroded, and their corrosion will be a witness against you and will eat your flesh like fire. You have heaped up treasure in the last days." **James 5:1-3**

"By covetousness they will exploit you with deceptive words; for a long time their judgment has not been idle, and their destruction does not slumber." **2 Peter 2:3**

"Do not love the world or the things in the world. If anyone loves the world, the love of the Father is not in him. For all that is in the world—the lust of the flesh, the lust of the eyes, and the pride of life—is not of the Father but is of the world. And the world is passing away, and the lust of it; but he who does the will of God abides forever." **1 John 2:15–17**

OVERCOMING SIN

"If your right eye causes you to sin, pluck it out and cast it from you; for it is more profitable for you that one of your members perish, than for your whole body to be cast into hell. And if your right hand causes you to sin, cut it off and cast it from you; for it is more profitable for you that one of your members perish, than for your whole body to be cast into hell." **Matthew 5:29–30**

"Watch and pray, lest you enter into temptation. The spirit indeed is willing, but the flesh is weak." **Matthew 26:41**

"Jesus answered them, 'Most assuredly, I say to you, whoever commits sin is a slave of sin. And a slave does not abide in the house forever, but a son abides forever. Therefore if the Son makes you free, you shall be free indeed.'" **John 8:34-36**

"These things I have spoken to you, that in Me you may have peace. In the world you will have tribulation; but be of good cheer, I have overcome the world." **John 16:33**

"Therefore do not let sin reign in your mortal body, that you should obey it in its lusts." **Romans 6:12**

"And having been set free from sin, you became slaves of righteousness." **Romans 6:18**

"For I know that in me (that is, in my flesh) nothing good dwells; for to will is present with me, but how to perform what is good I do not find." **Romans 7:18**

"There is therefore now no condemnation to those who are in Christ Jesus, who do not walk according to the flesh, but according to the Spirit. For the law of the Spirit of life in Christ Jesus has made me free from the law of sin and death." **Romans 8:1–2**

"For if you live according to the flesh you will die; but if by the Spirit you put to death the deeds of the body, you will live." **Romans 8:13**

"I beseech you therefore, brethren, by the mercies of God, that you present your bodies a living sacrifice, holy, acceptable to God, which is your reasonable service. And do not be conformed to this world, but be transformed by the renewing of your mind, that you may prove what is that good and acceptable and perfect will of God." **Romans 12:1–2**

"No temptation has overtaken you except such as is common to man; but God is faithful, who will not allow you to be tempted beyond what you are able, but with the temptation will also make the way of escape, that you may be able to bear it." **1 Corinthians 10:13**

"Therefore, if anyone is in Christ, he is a new creation; old things have passed away; behold, all things have become new." **2 Corinthians 5:17**

"Do not be deceived, God is not mocked; for whatever a man sows, that he will also reap. For he who sows to his flesh will of the flesh reap corruption, but he who sows to the Spirit will of the Spirit reap everlasting life." **Galatians 6:7–8**

"I say then: Walk in the Spirit, and you shall not fulfill the lust of the flesh." **Galatians 5:16**

"Do not be deceived, God is not mocked; for whatever a man sows, that he will also reap. For he who sows to his flesh will of the flesh reap corruption, but he who sows to the Spirit will of the Spirit reap everlasting life." **Galatians 6:7–8**

"That you put off, concerning your former conduct, the old man which grows corrupt according to the deceitful lusts, and be renewed in the spirit of your mind, and that you put on the new man which was created according to God, in true righteousness and holiness." **Ephesians 4:22–24**

"Brethren, I do not count myself to have apprehended; but one thing I do, forgetting those things which are behind and reaching forward to those things which are ahead, I press toward the goal for the prize of the upward call of God in Christ Jesus." **Philippians 3:13–14**

"Therefore put to death your members which are on the earth: fornication, uncleanness, passion, evil desire, and covetousness, which is idolatry." **Colossians 3:5**

"For the grace of God that brings salvation has appeared to all men, teaching us that, denying ungodliness and worldly lusts, we should live soberly, righteously, and godly in the present age." **Titus 2:11–12**

"But each one is tempted when he is drawn away by his own desires and enticed. Then, when desire has conceived, it gives birth to sin; and sin, when it is full-grown, brings forth death." **James 1:14–15**

"Therefore submit to God. Resist the devil and he will flee from you." **James 4:7**

"Who Himself bore our sins in His own body on the tree, that we, having died to sins, might live for righteousness—by whose stripes you were healed." **1 Peter 2:24**

"As His divine power has given to us all things that pertain to life and godliness, through the knowledge of Him who called us by glory and virtue, by which have been given to us exceedingly great and precious promises, that through these you may be partakers of the divine nature, having escaped the corruption that is in the world through lust." **2 Peter 1:3–4**

"If we confess our sins, He is faithful and just to forgive us our sins and to cleanse us from all unrighteousness." **1 John 1:9**

"Whoever abides in Him does not sin. Whoever sins has neither seen Him nor known Him." **1 John 3:6**

Endnotes

CHAPTER 1

1. Diogenes Laertius, *Live of Eminent Philosophers*, trans. C. D. Yonge, G. Bell and Sons, LTD. (Project Gutenberg, 2018), 224. https://www.gutenberg.org/files/57342/57342-h/57342-h.htm (accessed February 10, 2026).

CHAPTER 2

1. Plutarch, *Moralia*, Vol. XIII, Part 1, trans. Harold Cherniss, Loeb Classical Library, Harvard University Press, 1976. https://www.loebclassics.com/view/plutarch-moralia_control_anger/1939/pb_LCL337.93.xml (accessed February 10, 2016).

CHAPTER 3

1. Francis Bacon, *Essays: The Essays or Counsels, Civil and Moral, of Francis Ld. Verulam Viscount St. Albans* (Project Gutenberg, 2013), chap. Of Envy. https://www.gutenberg.org/files/575/575-h/575-h.htm (accessed February 10, 2026).
2. Horace, *Satires, Epistles, Art of Poetry*, trans. H. Rushton Fairclough, Loeb Classical Library, Harvard University Press, 1929. https://www.loebclassics.com/view/horace

-epistles/1926/pb_LCL194.267.xml (accessed February 10, 2016).
3. Samuel L. Johnson, *The Rambler, No. 183*, December 17, 1751. https://www.johnsonessays.com/the-rambler/no-183-the-influence-of-envy-and-interest-compared/ (accessed February 10, 2016).
4. Petronius Arbiter. *Petronius, Fragments*, trans. Michael Heseltine, William Heinemann Ltd., 1913. https://www.perseus.tufts.edu/hopper/text?doc=urn:cts:latinLit:phi0972.phi001f.perseus-eng1:25 (accessed February 10, 2016).
5. William Shakespeare, "The Merchant of Venice" Act 4, Scene 1, lines 125–26.

CHAPTER 4

1. "Sexual Activity and Contraceptive Use Among Teenagers in the United States, 2011–2015," National Center for Health Statistics, accessed February 10, 2025, https://www.cdc.gov/nchs/pressroom/nchs_press_releases/2017/201706_NSFG.htm.
2. William Cowper, "There Is a Fountain", 1772.

CHAPTER 7

1. Kingsley, Charles, *The Good News of God, Sermons* (MacMillan and Co., 1887).
2. Horace, *Satires, Epistles, Art of Poetry*, trans. H. Rushton Fairclough, Loeb Classical Library, Harvard University Press, 1929. https://www.loebclassics.com/view/horace-epistles/1926/pb_LCL194.267.xml (accessed February 10, 2016).

About the Author

BILLY GRAHAM (1918–2018), world-renowned preacher, evangelist, and author, delivered the gospel message to more people face-to-face than anyone in history and ministered on every continent of the world in almost 200 countries and territories. His ministry extended far beyond stadiums and arenas, utilizing radio, television, film, print media, wireless communications, and thirty-three books, all that still carry the Good News of God's redemptive love for everyone. Engraved on a simple fieldstone in the Memorial Prayer Garden where he is buried at the Billy Graham Library in Charlotte, North Carolina, these words exemplify how the man and the minister wished to be remembered: "Preacher of the Gospel of the Lord Jesus Christ."

Freedom from the Seven Deadly Sins

STEPS TO PEACE WITH GOD

1. God's Purpose: Peace and Life

God loves you and wants you to experience peace and life—abundant and eternal.

The Bible says ...

"We have peace with God through our Lord Jesus Christ." *Romans 5:1, NKJV*

"For God so loved the world that He gave His only begotten Son, that whoever believes in Him should not perish but have everlasting life." *John 3:16, NKJV*

"I have come that they may have life, and that they may have it more abundantly." *John 10:10, NKJV*

Since God planned for us to have peace and the abundant life right now, why are most people not having this experience?

2. Our Problem: Separation From God

God created us in His own image to have an abundant life. He did not make us as robots to automatically love and obey Him, but gave us a will and a freedom of choice.

We chose to disobey God and go our own willful way. We still make this choice today. This results in separation from God.

The Bible says ...

"For all have sinned and fall short of the glory of God." *Romans 3:23, NKJV*

"For the wages of sin is death, but the gift of God is eternal life in Christ Jesus our Lord." *Romans 6:23, NKJV*

Our choice results in separation from God.

OUR ATTEMPTS

Through the ages, individuals have tried in many ways to bridge this gap ... without success ...

THE BIBLE SAYS ...

"There is a way that seems right to a man, but its end is the way of death."
Proverbs 14:12, NKJV

"But your iniquities have separated you from your God; and your sins have hidden His face from you, so that He will not hear."
Isaiah 59:2, NKJV

There is only one remedy for this problem of separation.

3. GOD'S REMEDY: THE CROSS

Jesus Christ is the only answer to this problem. He died on the cross and rose from the grave, paying the penalty for our sin and bridging the gap between God and people.

THE BIBLE SAYS ...

"For there is one God and one Mediator between God and men, the Man Christ Jesus."
1 Timothy 2:5, NKJV

"For Christ also suffered once for sins, the just for the unjust, that He might bring us to God."
1 Peter 3:18, NKJV

"But God shows his love for us in that while we were still sinners, Christ died for us." *Romans 5:8, ESV*

God has provided the only way ... we must make the choice ...

STEPS TO PEACE WITH GOD

4. Our Response: Receive Christ

We must trust Jesus Christ and receive Him by personal invitation.

The Bible Says ...

"Behold, I stand at the door and knock. If anyone hears My voice and opens the door, I will come in to him and dine with him, and he with Me." *Revelation 3:20, NKJV*

"But to all who did receive him, who believed in his name, he gave the right to become children of God." *John 1:12, ESV*

"If you confess with your mouth that Jesus is Lord and believe in your heart that God raised him from the dead, you will be saved." *Romans 10:9, ESV*

Are you here ... or here?

Is there any good reason why you cannot receive Jesus Christ right now?

How to Receive Christ:

1. Admit your need (say, "I am a sinner").
2. Be willing to turn from your sins (repent) and ask for God's forgiveness.
3. Believe that Jesus Christ died for you on the cross and rose from the grave.
4. Through prayer, invite Jesus Christ to come in and control your life through the Holy Spirit (receive Jesus as Lord and Savior).

What to Pray:

> Dear God,
>   I know that I am a sinner. I want to turn from my sins, and I ask for Your forgiveness. I believe that Jesus Christ is Your Son. I believe He died for my sins and that You raised Him to life. I want Him to come into my heart and to take control of my life. I want to trust Jesus as my Savior and follow Him as my Lord from this day forward.
>
>   In Jesus' Name, amen.
>
> _____   _____
> Date   Signature

Freedom from the Seven Deadly Sins

God's Assurance: His Word

If you prayed this prayer, the Bible says …

"For 'everyone who calls on the name of the Lord will be saved.'"
Romans 10:13, ESV

Did you sincerely ask Jesus Christ to come into your life? Where is He right now? What has He given you?

"For by grace you have been saved through faith. And this is not your own doing; it is the gift of God, not a result of works, so that no one may boast." *Ephesians 2:8–9, ESV*

The Bible says …

"He who has the Son has life; he who does not have the Son of God does not have life. These things I have written to you who believe in the name of the Son of God, that you may know that you have eternal life, and that you may continue to believe in the name of the Son of God."
1 John 5:12–13, NKJV

Receiving Christ, we are born into God's family through the supernatural work of the Holy Spirit, who indwells every believer. This is called regeneration or the "new birth."

This is just the beginning of a wonderful new life in Christ. To deepen this relationship you should:

1. Read your Bible every day to know Christ better.
2. Talk to God in prayer every day.
3. Tell others about Christ.
4. Worship, fellowship, and serve with other Christians in a church where Christ is preached.
5. As Christ's representative in a needy world, demonstrate your new life by your love and concern for others.

God bless you as you do.

Franklin Graham

If you want further help in the decision you have made, write to:
Billy Graham Evangelistic Association
1 Billy Graham Parkway, Charlotte, NC 28201-0001

1-877-2GRAHAM (1-877-247-2426)
BillyGraham.org/commitment

A DYING WORLD NEEDS THE HOPE OF JESUS CHRIST.

There are more people alive today without the hope of Jesus than ever before. Together, let's reach them—in our communities and across the globe—with the Good News and tell them about "*the riches of the glory of this mystery, which is Christ in you, the hope of glory*" (Colossians 1:27, ESV). Since our founding in 1950, this has been our singular mission.

To find out how you can offer the hope of Christ to our lost and dying world, visit **BillyGraham.org** today.

BILLY GRAHAM
Evangelistic Association

Always Good News.

©2020 BGEA